UNPUBLISHABLE!

REJECTED WRITERS FROM JANE AUSTEN TO ZANE GREY

Elaine Borish, an American living in London, was born in New York City. She holds degrees from Rutgers, Boston University, and Northeastern University and has taught at universities in New England. In old England, she has lectured in English and American literature at Morley College in London. Her numerous articles have appeared in leading newspapers and magazines.

Also by Elaine Borish

A Legacy of Names
Literary Lodgings

Elaine Borish

———————————————

UNPUBLISHABLE!

REJECTED WRITERS FROM JANE AUSTEN TO ZANE GREY

Fidelio Press

Boulder • London

Published by
Fidelio Press
61 Pine Tree Lane
Boulder, Colorado 80304

ISBN 0-9524881-1-6

Printed in the United States of America.

Cover design by Allee Trendall

CONTENTS

Dedicated to those who have been published and to those seeking publication.

PREFACE

UNPUBLISHABLE! delves into the stories of over thirty authors of the past whose works, although initially rejected, are today very much alive. Their experiences of repudiation can only cheer and support readers.

Publishers' rejections must have defeated many a writer. Indeed, we have no way of knowing about those writers who encountered difficulties and gave up. But of writers who remained tenacious despite discouragement, we do know. Their accounts can only convey an encouraging message of hope to anyone who thinks about writing for publication. The story of a manuscript rebuffed by the literary establishment, a manuscript that later goes on to achieve recognition and success, is an inspiring one with a clear message about the value of confidence and perseverance.

Fortunately for English literature, many beloved and respected writers (who were not necessarily beloved or respected when they first submitted their manuscripts) persisted despite rejections of benighted publishers. How much poorer the world of letters would be if they had taken the easier road and given up. How frightening to conjecture how many talented people may actually have done just that.

Of course success stories prevail about the writer whose work is immediately recognized for the great piece of writing it is and published without much ado to great acclaim. D. H. Lawrence's first novel, *The White Peacock*, was accepted by the first publisher who saw it. E. M. Forster had well-deserved good luck when he sent his first novel, *Where Angels Fear to Tread*, to Blackwood's to query about serialization in their magazine, and they offered to publish it as a book.

But how many worthwhile manuscripts might just as easily never have come to light? How many worthy voices were silenced by the disheartening bluster of repudiation or condemnation? When Charlotte Brontë first considered authorship and wrote to the noted critic William Hazlitt for advice, she was admonished to direct her efforts toward being a good housekeeper. How much the literary world would have lost if she had heeded his advice. . . .

Consider how close Jane Austen came to oblivion! If she had deferred to the inaction of the publisher who kept *Northanger Abbey* (as *Susan)* for thirteen years with no intention of publishing it. . . . Or Beatrix Potter who, rejected by Warne, printed a private edition of her enormously successful story of Peter Rabbit before Warne later reconsidered and accepted. The list is endless.

Consider too how many works saw the light of day only because their authors paid for publication. Nor need anyone be put off by self-publishing (not to be confused with vanity publishing of a book that is of interest only to the writer at great profit only to the printer). Leonard and Virginia Woolf issued their own novels by their own Hogarth Press, which they founded in 1912, making one wonder: Who's afraid of self-publication?

A definitive volume revealing the stories of ALL the great writers who faced rejection is not possible, but surely some readers will have their own stories to add to a necessarily incomplete list.

JANE AUSTEN

"... there was not any time stipulated for its publication, neither are we bound to publish it."

Readers may be astonished to learn that one of the greatest writers in the history of English literature could ever have been rejected. Not only was her novel unwanted, but the rejection of *Pride and Prejudice* may have deprived the world of additional novels from the pen of Jane Austen.

Jane Austen was born on 16 December 1775 in the village of Steventon in Hampshire, where her father was rector. She had been writing since she was twelve and emerged from the juvenilia (which totals about twenty-nine pieces) ready to seek publication.

Of the six completed novels of Jane Austen, *Pride and Prejudice,* that great classic of the English language, represents her first work written for publication as well as her first rejection. After completing it in 1797, when she was twenty-two, she showed it to her father. The Reverend George Austen, also a classical scholar and a severe critic of her apprentice work, was extremely impressed with the manuscript that was originally entitled *First Impressions* and deemed it worthy of publication. He wrote to a London firm describing the three-volume novel and offering to pay the expenses of publication, a common and respectable practice at the time.

1

But Messrs. Cadell did not deem it worthy even of being read and declined to look at it. By rejecting Jane Austen, they may have done a service to literary history, some believe, for her mature pen revised and renamed it and created the perfect masterpiece in *Pride and Prejudice* sixteen years later. Perhaps. But perhaps it is just as likely that with appropriate recognition, her career would have started sooner and produced more than the small output of six novels. After Cadell's refusal, she did not again try for publication for another half dozen years. In any case, Cadell lives in infamy as the man who was too busy with current Gothic thrillers, epitomized by Mrs. Radcliff's *The Mysteries of Udolpho,* to be bothered with *Pride and Prejudice.*

The rebuff that came in November 1797 must have greatly disappointed the would-be author, for she put away for a few years the manuscript of *Elinor and Marianne* (later *Sense and Sensibility*) on which she was working. However, even more disheartening than her first rejection must have been her first acceptance.

Northanger Abbey, begun in 1798 under the title *Susan,* satirized popular Gothic romances of the day. The first of Jane Austen's six major novels to be accepted, it was sold in 1803 on behalf of the anonymous author to a London publisher for ten pounds. But what transpired was more outrageous than outright rejection would have been. Although Crosby and Company had advertised it in a list of forthcoming books, this book was not forthcoming. For unknown reasons, the publisher changed his mind, and it was not published—at least not in her lifetime.

After six years of inaction had elapsed, she wrote to the firm under a pseudonym inquiring about its fate and offering to replace it if lost. The publisher replied that he was under no obligation to print it and would not release the copyright as ". . . there was not any time stipulated for its publication, neither are we bound to publish it." He threatened legal action—"we shall take proceedings to stop the sale"—if the author attempted to publish the manuscript elsewhere. He would, however, willingly return the manuscript if the novelist would return his ten-pound investment. Her limited income made it necessary to decline the offer.

Not until 1816 did she manage to retrieve it with the help of her brother's negotiations. Henry Austen went to the offices of Messrs. Crosby and paid ten pounds to extricate the neglected manuscript and the copyright from their hands. Only when the transaction was complete did he have the satisfaction of revealing that the manuscript the firm had kept for thirteen years with no intention of publishing was written by the author of *Pride and Prejudice, Mansfield Park,* and *Emma.*

Sense and Sensibility—Elinor and Marianne was its earlier version—was her first published novel. Mr. Thomas Egerton of London, from whose presses it emerged in 1811 with "By a Lady" on the title page, took little risk. Although Jane Austen did not make payment of a specified sum to cover costs of printing, she did agree to reimburse him for any loss he might incur. Happily, sales covered expenses, and the first edition of about a thousand copies sold out in twenty months, bringing her a profit of £140.

Now she was ready to take up *First Impressions* and in November 1812 submitted the completed manuscript to Mr. Egerton. He accepted with alacrity, paying her outright the rather niggardly sum of £110 for the copyright but with no requirement this time that she meet expenses. It appeared in 1813 as *Pride and Prejudice* by the anonymous author of *Sense and Sensibility.*

Mansfield Park followed in May 1814, again published by Egerton, again anonymously, and the first edition sold out by August. Such was the fame of *Pride and Prejudice* and

Mansfield Park that her next book was taken on by the eminent Mr. John Murray, founder of the *Quarterly Review* and publisher of such notable authors as Lord Byron—a tribute to the successful author. Her popularity inevitably made her anonymity an open secret. One admirer of the novels written "By a Lady" was the Prince of Wales. He discovered her identity through his physician who was attending the seriously ill Henry Austen while Jane was with her brother in London. The Prince Regent invited her to tour Carlton House, and he invited her to dedicate her next book to him. The hint was correctly construed as a command, and when *Emma* appeared in December 1815, the dedication, despite her adverse feelings toward his dissolute life style, was to George IV by "His Royal Highness's Dutiful and Obedient Humble Servant, the Author."

She made good earnings on *Emma*, published on 16 December 1815, her fortieth birthday, and the last book to appear in her lifetime. Total earnings in her lifetime amounted to under £700. In 1816 Jane Austen completed *Persuasion*, but it was published posthumously, together with *Northanger Abbey*.

Jane Austen's health was failing in 1817. She was suffering from an illness that took its inexorable course. She did not revise the manuscript of *Northanger Abbey* but apologized to readers in an 'Advertisement' that the book had been intended for publication in 1803 and parts may have been rendered obsolete by changes which have occurred in the world since then. Her preface in the 1818 edition also contained these words: "That any bookseller should think it worth while to purchase what he did not think it worth while to publish seems extraordinary."

The year 1817 marks the untimely death of Jane Austen at the age of forty-two. She had left her home in Chawton for Winchester to secure treatment for a condition unidentified and untreatable then but diagnosed in modern times as Addison's disease. There she died on the 18th of July. Illness had kept her from revising works or completing *Sanditon*, the novel on which she was working. Both *Northanger Abbey* and *Persuasion* were published posthumously in 1818.

As it is a truth universally acknowledged that Jane Austen is one of the greatest novelists in the English language, any outrage felt by rebuffs to her works might be met by her own famous statement in *Mansfield Park*: "I quit such odious subjects as soon as I can." But we do not quit. We go on to uncover further examples of publishing mismanagement, misjudgment, and maltreatment.

J. M. BARRIE

He lost £25 on the publication of his first
novel, *Better Dead*.

When J. M. Barrie left Edinburgh University after receiving a
degree in 1882, he was determined to be a writer and had
already completed a three-volume novel entitled *A Child of
Nature*. The novel, written when he was a youth at Dumfries
Academy, was submitted to a publisher who showed true
publishing perspicacity when he innocently referred to the
writer as a "clever lady." Less innocently, he offered to
produce it if the author would pay £100. Barrie could hardly
afford that sum at the time and came away wounded by
the mistaken identity but with his determination to be an
author intact. "The malignancy of publishers," he said, "could
not turn me back. . . literature was my game." Some forty-
five years later he came upon that early manuscript and
destroyed it.

Bent on authorship, he began, like so many great authors,
with journalism. While at university, he had written freelance
drama and literary criticism for Edinburgh papers. Afterwards, he joined the staff of the *Nottingham Journal*, which he
was later to disguise as the *Silchester Mirror* in *When a Man's
Single*, his 1887 novel of journalistic life.

His aim was to get to London. He submitted articles and
sketches regularly to London papers, and most were just as

regularly returned. Some articles he sent to the editor of *St. James's Gazette*, and Frederick Greenwood scribbled on the back of one, "But I liked that Scotch thing. Any more of those?"

Those words opened a magic mine of material to be excavated from Kirriemuir, his place of birth on 9 May 1860. That Scotch thing was his first article on the Auld Lichts and a signpost on the road to success, as those Scotch things were eventually collected and printed as *Auld Licht Idylls*. He had found the lode as his mother enabled him to create quaint stories of humble Scottish life by reviving her old memories of Kirriemuir; auld licht topics made their way into London papers. After "An Auld Licht Community" came an auld licht marriage, a funeral, courtship, scandal . . . . Encouraged, he wrote to Greenwood asking whether he should come to London. A prompt reply strongly advised him to remain at home in Scotland. But the London call was too powerful, and Barrie just as promptly left for London on 28 March 1885.

Just two years later, Barrie was ready with his first book. But the publishers were not. Greenwood, who considered Barrie a personal discovery, gave him letters of introduction. Despite the influential recommendation, publishers refused to take the risk. *Better Dead* did not find its way into print until finally it was taken on by Swan, Sonnenschein, Lowrie & Co. of Paternoster Row, but at the author's expense. Issued in November 1887, and priced at one shilling, the book could not possibly yield a profit unless it became a best seller. Barrie lost £25 over the transaction. However, with its colored cover and the crucial words "by J. M. Barrie," the novel did yield a gratifying result. It made him an author. Barrie later confessed to maintaining a sentimental interest in *Better Dead*, his first novel.

Following that small volume came *Auld Licht Idylls*, a collection of sketches and stories he had written for *St. James's Gazette* and other papers. The process was a common one among nineteenth-century novelists who had begun their careers as journalists. Dickens, for example, had gathered old pieces for inclusion in *Sketches by Boz.*

Although *Auld Licht Idylls* was published by Hodder and Stoughton in April 1888 to a chorus of rapturous praise, it had not been snatched up by those to whom it was offered. Many others had refused it, even as a gift. Fortunately, Hodder and Stoughton saw its merits and also the merits of his novel which followed, *When a Man's Single*, which they published by the end of that year. Barrie went on working on articles, which now sold easily, and his career moved swiftly ahead.

An Edinburgh Eleven (1889) further exploited his success with Scottish character sketches. The slim volume of past sketches from *The British Weekly* caused less than a sensation. And Barrie offended the people of Kirriemuir who felt they were being ridiculed and their customs exaggerated as Barrie capitalized on their town to which he gave the fictional name of Thrums (an archaic term for the bunch of loose threads which hung beside the handloom for repairing broken threads in the fabric). Just seven months later appeared the book which carried him to fame, the highly-acclaimed *A Window in Thrums.*

With the appearance of *The Little Minister* in the autumn of 1891, he arrived. The sentimental novel was dramatized six years afterwards and became a sensational success on the stage. He enjoyed further success with a biography of his mother, *Margaret Ogilvy* (1896), the novel *Sentimental Tommy* (1896), and its sequel, *Tommy and Grizel* (1900).

Having begun his career using journalism as a gateway to literary fame, the writer of good novels turned to drama, and his great plays insured his immortality. Apart from the vastly appealing and ever-popular *Peter Pan*, which has made him known throughout the world, are *Quality Street, What Every Woman Knows, The Admirable Chrichton, Dear Brutus, Mary*

Rose, and *The Boy David,* produced shortly before his death in June 1937.

Once, during rehearsals of *Peter Pan,* one of the child actresses asked, "What makes you write, Mr. Barrie?" He answered, "Why, don't you know, Nibs? My fingers are full of ink, and it *must* come out." But before it came out, it is worthwhile recalling that before the world understood or accepted the genius of J. M. Barrie, he himself had to pay for publication of his first book.

L. FRANK BAUM

> The grounds for rejection were that
> children were already content with the
> fairy tales available to them and that if a
> profitable market for an American fairy
> tale existed, it would have been written
> long ago.

The author of one of the most endearing and enduring books of all time—*The Wonderful Wizard of Oz*—started life on 15 May 1856 as Lyman Frank Baum in a small village some fifteen miles east of Syracuse, New York. As a young man he tried a variety of vocations. Infatuated with the theatre, he had several flings as an actor. He became a salesman and a journalist. After his marriage in 1882, he moved west to the Dakota Territory and opened a general notions store called Baum's Bazaar. Then he became owner and columnist for the local newspaper and, when that failed, resettled in Chicago, where he worked on a newspaper before becoming a crockery buyer and traveling salesman.

He kept changing careers, but the one thing that never changed was his delight in entertaining children. He amused them by embellishing Mother Goose verses and transforming them into stories until he eventually had a manuscript. The new publishing firm of Way and Williams encouraged new writers and accepted Baum's *Mother Goose in Prose*. The beautifully-printed volume that appeared in 1897 was popular enough to be reprinted several times.

At the age of forty-one, Baum started publication of *The Show Window*, a monthly trade magazine for merchants and professionals that first appeared on 1 November 1897. He sold the profitable venture in 1902.

At the Chicago Press Club, Baum met William Denslow, an artist who became his partner. Denslow drew illustrations for some amusing verses Baum had written. Seeking publication, Baum took the illustrated jingles to the George M. Hill Company. Hill liked it, but his production manager did not, while his head salesman felt that with a catchy title it might sell a small edition of five thousand. After much quibbling, after Baum's suggested title of *Father Goose* and the salesman's emendation to *Father Goose, His Book*, Hill, as president, made the final decision. They would *not* undertake publication at all.

Hill was, however, willing to print, bind, and sell a small edition if Baum and Denslow would pay for it. Despite having little money, the two men managed to find the means, and *Father Goose* was published on 25 September 1899. To Hill's astonishment, it sold out so quickly that a second edition of 10,000 copies was printed on 16 October. By the end of the year 75,000 copies had been printed of the juvenile sensation of the year.

Success with *Father Goose* made Baum consider putting into print the story of Dorothy and the Scarecrow, which he had been telling to children. Once, while indulging in the pleasure of narrating tales to a youthful audience, he was interrupted by a young neighbor wanting to know where the Scarecrow and the Tin Woodman lived. Baum looked carefully around the room and came up with the answer—the Land of Oz. But where is the Land of Oz, persisted his seven-year-old son Kenneth. The child might not have been

11

pleased to learn that its precise location was on the bottom drawer of a filing cabinet. Baum had looked around and seen on the top drawer of the cabinet the letters A-N and on the bottom drawer, O-Z.

Although he was busy with *Show Window* magazine, Baum began the book called *The Emerald City*. Denslow drew sketches. By the autumn of 1899 they were able to submit several chapters to Hill, who kept it for six weeks before declining and advising that children were content with fairy tales already available to them and that their parents, the potential purchasers, would not buy anything as unconventional as an American fairy tale.

They took *The Emerald City* to other publishers and got other rejections. One turned it down commenting that if there were a need for it, the fairy tale would have been produced long ago.

In Hill's office one day to pick up the royalty check for *Father Goose*, Baum and Denslow got into an argument with Hill over *The Emerald City*. Hill expressed the view that black and white drawings suffice for a child's book and that color illustrations were an unnecessary extravagance. Then he made a proposal. If they felt so strongly about their own views, why not take the gamble of putting up the money for color illustrations, type setting, and printing and binding of a few thousand copies, as they had done for *Father Goose*. Baum and Denslow took up the challenge and decided to invest *Father Goose* royalties in *The Emerald City*. But the production head insisted on another title, and it evolved from *The Fairyland of Oz* to *The Land of Oz* and finally to *The Wonderful Wizard of Oz.*

What happened after publication on 1 August 1900 was sheer wizardry. A first edition of ten thousand soon sold out. Twenty-five thousand more were printed in October, thirty thousand in November, and twenty-five thousand in January 1901—a total of ninety thousand. The best seller of 1900 became a best seller of all time. It became a stage play and a film, and it continues to entertain and intrigue.

That Baum had gone through a number of vocations in search of the vocation that he eventually found within himself, the gift of story telling, is just one of several curiosities. While the book continued to show vitality, the George M. Hill Company did not and went into bankruptcy in February 1902. The Baum-Denslow partnership broke up. But Baum continued telling stories and capitalized on the world of Oz in an additional thirteen books including *The Road to Oz* (1909), *Dorothy and the Wizard of Oz* (1908), and *The Emerald City of Oz* (1910). However, none approached the pinnacle of success reached by the first Oz book, *The Wonderful Wizard of Oz*, initially refused by publishing wizards.

CHARLOTTE BRONTË

"... deficient in startling incident...
would never suit the circulating
libraries."

Charlotte Brontë's story of rejection begins with her own rejection of the advice proffered by Robert Southey. In 1836, in search of an alternative career to the drudgery of life as a teacher or governess, she wrote to the poet laureate asking about the possibilities that existed for a woman writer and the outlook for earning a living by it. He advised her against pursuing a career of letters: "Literature cannot be the business of a woman's life, and it ought not be. ..." But why then, having sought his counsel, did she go on?

Despite harsh surroundings and the hard life at Haworth Parsonage, talent and imagination flourished in the Brontë home, and each of the three Brontë sisters had delved into some writing. In 1845 Charlotte was so excited by her discovery of a notebook containing Emily's "vigorous and genuine" poems that she was propelled into a publishing scheme. She had saved many of her own poems, and Anne too had been writing excellent poetry. Why not make a selection of poems by all three sisters and send them off?

Charlotte queried Messrs. Chambers of Edinburgh for guidance on how to proceed, and they suggested submitting the unknown poems to the small firm of Aylott & Jones. Her letter of inquiry on the 28th of January 1846 received an encouraging reply, and she submitted the completed manuscript in February. The authors had to bear the cost of thirty pounds toward the production of the volume but considered themselves fortunate in being able to apply a part of their aunt's legacy toward that sum. They agreed also to adopt pseudonyms to escape prejudice against female writers. In May 1846, appeared a slim green volume of fifty-one poems entitled *Poems* by Currer, Ellis, and Acton Bell.

By the middle of July, sales soared to a grand total of two copies. Although warmly praised by the critics, the book was simply a failure. Nevertheless, the poets were undaunted. Charlotte wrote in later years, "Ill-success failed to crush us." The three wanted desperately now to become successful authors. Resolved to publish, they turned to the serious purpose of novels and indeed had already begun writing fiction.

For her first novel, *The Professor*, Charlotte adapted her own unhappy experience in Brussels, where she had gone as a pupil-teacher and fallen miserably and hopelessly in love with the married director of the French school.

By the end of June, Charlotte had completed *The Professor*; Emily, *Wuthering Heights*; and Anne, *Agnes Grey*. They set out to find a publisher for the novels in the fashionable three-volume format. Aylott & Jones, who had taken on their poetry, did not publish fiction but supplied a list of possibilities who might put them on the road to fame and fortune. Or so they thought.

The triple manuscript was rejected again and again until finally, in July 1847, Thomas Cautley Newby came through. However, he offered to consider only *Wuthering Heights* and *Agnes Grey*, not *The Professor*. Moreover, his terms required Emily and Anne to bear the cost of £50 for production of an edition of 350 copies. The good news was that if successful, and if reprinted, part of their investment would be refunded.

Charlotte urged her sisters to accept the unacceptable terms. Despite the blow to her own prospects, she remained undeterred from her purpose and had already begun *Jane Eyre*. Even a sixth rejection of *The Professor* brought her, not despair, but comfort and hope in the sympathetic words of Mr. William Smith Williams, a reader of the minor publishing firm of Smith Elder and Company of Cornhill. He recognized the strength and power of the manuscript and invited her to submit another work in the popular three-volume format.

This time she was ready. The three-volume novel that she posted on 24 August 1847 was *Jane Eyre*. What enormous excitement and enthusiasm it aroused! Mr. Smith read the manuscript in a single day and was astounded. The firm dealt honestly with her and published it within six weeks of acceptance, on 16 October 1847, to instant acclaim. In fact, Newby, who had not yet published her sisters' novels, capitalized on the fame of Currer Bell and quickly released *Wuthering Heights* by Ellis Bell and *Agnes Grey* by Acton Bell.

Jane Eyre became an instant best seller and received generally very favorable reviews. The enthusiastic critic of the *Examiner* reported that it was a book of such "decided power" that it could not have been written by a woman.

It was soon reprinted with the second edition dedicated to Thackeray, who called this honor "the greatest compliment I have ever received in my life." A third printing came in April. A complete triumph, it earned altogether about £500 for Charlotte, whose dream of authorship was now fulfilled.

But *The Professor* never found a publisher in her lifetime. It remained unacceptable by those who maintained that "it was deficient in startling incident" and "thrilling excitement" and therefore "would never suit the circulating libraries." *The Professor* did not appear before the public until June 1857. By that time, Charlotte—successful author, literary celebrity, happy wife, and expectant mother—had succumbed to the same disease that had caused the deaths of Emily and Anne. Charlotte died of consumption on 31 March 1855 at the age of thirty-nine.

Nowadays, critics find positive things to say about *The Professor*. And readers may well wonder whether the author was recalling Southey's attitude when she gave the manipulating directress of the school these discouraging words to speak of a distinguished student: ". . .it appears to me that ambition, *literary* ambition especially, is not a feeling to be cherished in the mind of a woman." The imperious character goes on to inquire whether the gifted young woman would not be "much safer and happier if taught to believe that in the quiet discharge of social duties consists her real vocation, than if stimulated to aspire after applause and publicity?"

Fortunately for posterity, Charlotte Brontë's perseverance and aspiration resulted in an immeasurable contribution to literature. Perhaps Jane Eyre's words express the author's own strong will in not heeding Southey's initial advice and persisting in the fight for publication: "I will be myself."

ELIZABETH BARRETT BROWNING

"... the work of an inexperienced
imagination"

Elizabeth Barrett Browning's first publication was a long epic poem entitled *The Battle of Marathon.* Seeing it in print produced in her the firm decision to change from the simple enjoyment of writing poetry (as she had been doing since the age of nine) to actually becoming a poet. To her proud father was due the gratitude for the appearance of the volume—a private edition of fifty copies. She was fourteen.

The following year, 1821, was the year of the onset of an illness that doctors were at a loss to accurately diagnose or treat. She was sent away from her Hope End home in the hills of Herefordshire to the Gloucester Spa to convalesce. Doctors further advised that she curtail reading and writing as these activities might exacerbate her debilitated condition. She nevertheless continued to indulge in the only pursuits that gave pleasure and meaning to her life and wrote at the time: "Literature was the star which in prospect illuminated my future days. . . the very soul of my being." The year 1821 also marks her first magazine publication, "Stanzas, Excited by Some Reflections on the Present State of Greece" in the *New Monthly Magazine.*

Despite continuing weakness and ill health, she sought recognition and appreciation from others, beyond relatives and friends. Publication in periodicals might bring her to the attention of outsiders, she believed, and, longing to be included in the circle of established poets, continued to write. In 1822 Henry Colburn of the *New Monthly Magazine* turned down one of her submissions. Later that year Thomas Campbell of the same magazine turned down her poems as "the work of an inexperienced imagination." Unchastised and unsquelched, she responded by sending him another poem, which received a curt rejection. Still undaunted, she went on writing.

Just after her twentieth birthday, in March 1826, *An Essay on Mind, with Other Poems* was published, again with private funds. Again, it was fervently admired by family and friends. But she needed the company and recognition of poets and strangers. Some small success in publication was hers to enjoy when her translation of Aeschylus' *Prometheus Bound* appeared in 1833, although A. J. Valpy had issued it without her name.

Her health continued to be frail even after the Barretts settled in 1838 into the London house so famously associated with them, 50 Wimpole Street. Soon after she was happily established in her new home came her first great publishing success, *The Seraphim, and Other Poems,* issued on 6 June to generally favorable critical reviews. But, alas, the year of the breakthrough to literary fame was also the year of the breakdown of her feeble health. She was forbidden to write and was sent to the warmer climes of Torquay, where she longed only to return to London.

Back in London and confined to Wimpole Street, she worked on her poetry and had four volumes published by 1842. When she submitted a new collection of poems to Edward Moxon, the great Victorian publisher of poetry was unwilling to take on the volume. He believed it lacked commercial value, although she was then one of the famous poets of the era. Perhaps the great man can be understood for turning down the opportunity to publish Elizabeth's poems, for apparently he even showed some reluctance to publish Wordsworth.

Rather than approach another publisher, Elizabeth decided to wait a year, write some additional poems, and try again. Almost immediately following Moxon's rejection, she had the satisfaction of being requested by a New York editor to send him some poems that he might extend her reputation in America.

In 1844 she was ready with a new volume entitled *Poems*. This time Moxon was also ready, and the handsome two-volume edition which appeared in August 1844 changed her life completely.

One of the poems of the collection, "Lady Geraldine's Courtship," led to her own courtship. It contained a compliment to Robert Browning, whose position and popularity as a major poet was not then so well established as her own. Her hero reads to his lady from a variety of poets and refers favorably to the work of the unknown Browning.

In January 1845, when Browning wrote the first of nearly six hundred letters that passed between them, he was thirty-two and she was thirty-eight. The mutual respect and friendship deepened into love after they met for the first time the following May. His guidance and encouragement had a salubrious effect on her health. They were married in September 1845, eloped to Italy, and lived happily in Florence, writing poetry, until she died peacefully in his arms on 29 June 1861.

ANTHONY BURGESS

". . . too Catholic and too guilt-ridden."

Not until he was in his forties did John Anthony Burgess Wilson, the author of over twenty novels, turn to writing as a profession. Born in Manchester, England, in 1917 and educated at Manchester University, Burgess served in the army in World War II, from 1940 to 1946. The last three of those years of military life he spent on Gibraltar.

Back in civilian life Burgess found that, although he had hoped for a career in music and had composed various chamber pieces, orchestral works, and incidental music for plays, he needed to exorcise the Gibraltar experience as well as test his ability to write a long prose work without getting bored. After four years as a teacher in a Banbury grammar school, he left England in 1954 to accept teaching positions in Malaya and in Borneo. It was during that period in the East that he produced his first published novels and began a literary career.

But Burgess had actually written his first novel, *A Vision of Battlements*, in 1949. Based on his Gibraltar experience of army life, it was not published until 1965. He had submitted the manuscript to William Heinemann before leaving for Malaya. Heinemann accepted, but attached a curious condition to the acceptance. They would publish it only as a

21

second novel. Burgess, who never had a problem with fecundity, complied with *The Worm and the Ring*, based on the grammar school experience in Banbury. But Roland Gant of Heinemann rejected also the second novel because it was "too Catholic and too guilt-ridden." (It was eventually published in 1961.)

His experiences in Malaya became the background for his next three novels—*Time for a Tiger* (1956), *The Enemy in the Blanket* (1958), and *Beds in the East* (1959)—his *Malayan Trilogy*. As an education officer with the British Colonial Service, it was more discreet to use a pseudonym for his fictional account of actual events and personalities, and he became Anthony Burgess.

Thus it was that his first written novel appeared sixteen years after he completed it and after his reputation was well established. Burgess wrote in the Introduction to the 1965 edition of *A Vision of Battlements* that "the typescript travelled to Malaya and Borneo with me, then back to England."

Burgess had returned to England because of illness. Diagnosed with a brain tumor and given a year to live, he decided to write books, an activity that would give him pleasure and also serve as something of a legacy for his wife. He produced five novels in one prolific year. To conceal his productivity, as a large output might be frowned upon by critics, two were issued under the pseudonym of Joseph Kell. Happily, there was no tumor, but the misdiagnosis changed his life as he took on a career as a writer.

Of his novels, *A Clockwork Orange* (1962) is undoubtedly the most famous, owing to the Stanley Kubrick film version. Among his other novels are *The Doctor Is*

Sick (1960), *One Hand Clapping* (1961), *Inside Mr. Enderby* (1963), *Nothing Like the Sun* (1964), *Enderby Outside* (1968), and *Earthly Powers* (1980). In addition, he wrote stories, articles, essays, reviews and at least fifteen non-fiction books on literature. *Here Comes Everybody* (1965) is an introduction to the work of James Joyce. *The Novel Now* (1967) discusses contemporary fiction. Burgess also wrote television scripts, translations, and a Broadway musical. When he died in 1993 at seventy-six, the man who could not at first be published, left a great number of great published works.

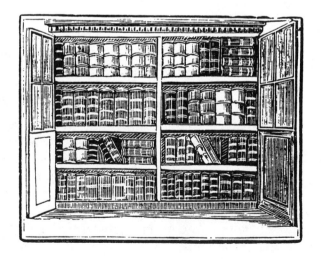

WILLA CATHER

A vanity press published her first book.

Willa Cather's first book was a volume of poems, *April Twilights*, published in 1903. She had been writing verse ever since her university days, and her poems had appeared in undergraduate magazines, then in national magazines.

At the University of Nebraska in Lincoln, she enrolled in a journalism course given by the young managing editor of the Nebraska *State Journal*, Will Owen Jones. He recognized her skill and invited her to write a regular column. After graduation in 1895, she continued to write for the *Journal* and for the *Courier* in Lincoln before moving to Pittsburgh to accept a position as assistant editor for a new magazine; she worked first at the *Home Monthly*, then on the Pittsburgh *Daily Leader*.

Her first foray into publication ended fruitlessly. Of the varied subjects she had been writing for various papers and periodicals, drama criticism was her most enjoyable. She compiled a series of open letters to actors, often degrading them and admonishing them on how to play their roles, which she hoped would be her first book. But publishers did not take to the idea, perhaps disliking the haughty tone with its strong and tactless opinions. The manuscript with the tentative title of *The Player Letters* reposed with a few publishers before being innocuously withdrawn.

Her name came to the attention of a Boston publisher who expressed an interest in her work and wanted to publish a volume of her poetry. Richard Badger urged her to make a selection of her verse and become part of the series of new poets he was running. Of course she accepted the proposal. The slim volume of poetry, typical of the debut of many an aspiring writer, appeared in April 1903.

The story of her publication sounds like an author's dream of instant success. But the fact is that she had to pay a specified sum of money to appear in print, for Richard Badger was the head of a vanity press. Although she had hoped to make a modest profit, sales were disappointing, and she probably never recovered her investment. She did manage to receive some favorable reviews, but under such an imprint the volume received scant attention. Nevertheless, she was now a poet in print. Afterwards, she turned to fiction, writing only sixteen more poems in the remainder of her life.

April 1903 has to be recorded as a turning point in the life of Willa Cather, for at the very same time that *April Twilights* appeared, *McClure's Magazine* began to show an interest in her. *McClure's* was a successful enterprise with a fine reputation for fiction. It was run by the energetic and enthusiastic S. S. McClure who had a talent for finding talent as he scoured Europe and America in search of writers for his magazine and publishing syndicate. He convinced Stevenson and Kipling to write for him, and he published Arnold Bennett and Arthur Conan Doyle as well as Mark Twain, Walt Whitman, and Julia Ward Howe.

That year he sent his cousin to the provinces in search of new authors for the McClure Syndicate. In Nebraska, Will Owen Jones strongly recommended Willa Cather. McClure asked to see her stories, and the investigation resulted in an imperious telegram from S. S. McClure summoning Willa Cather to come immediately to New York. She arrived as soon as she was able at the offices on West Twenty-third Street, and the two met on the first day of May. They talked at length, and S. S. McClure was wild with enthusiasm. He even took her home to Westchester to meet his family. McClure offered to publish her stories in book form. He would print them first in his magazine and in other journals if there was no room. He simply wanted to be the publisher for everything she wrote from then on.

Then she told him—and this is the astonishing fact—that she had already sent some of her stories to *McClure's*, and they had been rejected. McClure's response must have visited upon Willa Cather the dream of sweet revenge that every rejected writer fantasizes about. He called in to the interview the readers who had turned her down and demanded an explanation, chastising them for not having recognized or appreciated her ability. It must have been an immensely gratifying scene for the now-respected writer.

If he was elated by his discovery, she was delirious with happiness. She was launched as a writer. Never again would she be anxious about rejection slips.

McClure published her first collection of seven stories, *The Troll Garden*, in 1905. The following year, she accepted his offer of a job as associate editor on his magazine; she gave up her teaching position in Pittsburgh and moved to New York. With publication in 1912 of her first novel, *Alexander's Bridge*, the long apprenticeship was over. She was thirty-nine, perhaps a late start, but was soon to achieve widespread fame. She left her successful career at *McClure's Magazine* to devote her time entirely to writing.

When Willa Cather died on 24 April 1947, she left behind a legacy of great novels including: *O Pioneers!* (1913), *My Antonia* (1918), the Pulitzer prize-winning *One of Ours* (1922), *A Lost Lady* (1923), *The Professor's House* (1925), *My Mortal Enemy* (1926), and *Death Comes for the Archbishop* (1927).

Her position in American letters was increasingly recognized. She was awarded honorary degrees from Columbia University, Yale, University of California, and Princeton. But perhaps the greatest tribute of all was paid by Sinclair Lewis. Awarded the Nobel Prize, he stated that she should have had the coveted honor and that he would give nine Nobel prizes to have written *Death Comes for the Archbishop*.

AGATHA CHRISTIE

After making the rounds of half a dozen
publishers, her first novel finally found
acceptance, after a four-year search.

How Agatha Christie began a career as a writer of mystery
novels is no mystery, for she describes it in her
autobiography. She took up a challenge that came from her
older sister—"I bet you can't write a good detective
story"—and produced what has been called "one of the finest
firsts ever written."

For her first detective novel, *The Mysterious Affair at
Styles,* she created a clever and eccentric Belgian detective,
affected and pompous, an egghead with an egg-shaped head
and exotic mustache—the unforgettable Hercule Poirot. The
book took four years to find a willing publisher and did not
appear before the public until 1920.

First Hodder and Stoughton refused it. She sent it out
again, and it was again returned. Methuen also returned it,
saying that it was "not quite suitable" for their list. The
manuscript made the rounds of half a dozen publishers before
it was sent to The Bodley Head. There it remained for
eighteen months until John Lane, the managing director,
finally contacted the author to discuss her manuscript. It had
possibilities he believed, but needed alterations. Agatha made

the necessary changes, replacing the court scene of the last chapter with a conversation in the library.

She was delighted with the agreement they reached but, while awaiting publication, became impatient and expressed concern about whether it was ever coming out as she was already finishing a second one. Indeed, books continued to flow with amazing regularity from the pen of the prolific author.

However, she need not have been pleased with the contract, for she earned the paltry sum of £26 (her share of a magazine serial sale) on *The Mysterious Affair at Styles*. The Bodley Head contract also stipulated an option on her next five books: *The Secret Adversary* (1922), *Murder on the Links* (1923), *The Man in the Brown Suit* (1924), a collection of short stories called *Poirot Investigates* (1924), *The Secret of Chimneys* (1925).

With her 1926 masterpiece, *The Murder of Roger Ackroyd*, she changed publishers but continued to average at least a book a year. "A sausage machine, a perfect sausage machine," she has called herself. During her lifetime—Dame Agatha died in 1976 at the age of eighty-six—she produced over ninety titles.

Agatha Christie became the most financially successful author of all time, outselling even Shakespeare and earning more on royalties than any other writer. Her success has been phenomenal, with over two billion copies of her books sold worldwide in over one hundred languages. It is sobering to reflect that despite the unsurpassed and envious achievement, she had to endure unpleasant repudiation at the start of her career.

ARTHUR CONAN DOYLE

"It's too long—and too short—for the
Cornhill Magazine."

Before he became a writer, Arthur Conan Doyle studied medicine at Edinburgh University. There he met Dr. Joseph Bell, a skilled surgeon whose very appearance—forehead, sharp nose, hard chin—suggested pure reason. The good surgeon was to have a distinct influence on Conan Doyle's later literary career.

After qualifying as a doctor, Doyle set up in medical practice in Portsmouth, where he followed his vocation for eight years, and undertook the long struggle of waiting for patients. With plenty of spare time on hand, he indulged in writing—and undertook the long struggle of waiting for publishers.

He took the craft of writing more seriously than he had as a student, when he produced several undistinguished stories that appeared in a variety of periodicals. The stories he had written between 1878 and 1883 yielded no more than fifteen pounds a year. When "Habakuk Jephson's Statement" was accepted in 1883 by James Payn of the *Cornhill*, a prestigious magazine founded by Thackeray, it was considered a great breakthrough. He sent other stories to Payn, and most were returned.

But no publisher ever got a chance to reject his novel, *The Narrative of John Smith*, for it was lost by the post office the first time he sent it out. Another novel, *The Firm of Girdlestone*, begun in 1884, underwent a round of rejections and was not published until much later.

The literary scene changed for Conan Doyle when, reverting to his days as a medical student, he created a detective-character whose methods were reminiscent of those of Dr. Bell. As Sherrinford Hope evolved to become Sherlock Holmes (in deference to Oliver Wendell Holmes, the poet and medical pioneer whom he greatly admired), as Ormond Sacker became Dr. John H. Watson, and as *A Tangled Skein* became *A Study in Scarlet*, Arthur Conan Doyle became the creator of one of the most celebrated characters in English literature.

A Study in Scarlet is the important novel that first brought into being Sherlock Holmes and Dr. Watson, characters who would become world famous. From this book emanated countless other books, plays, radio and television programs, and industries producing every sort of ephemera from deerstalker caps to finger puppets. The book produced also a tourist industry with fans seeking out, then as now, the fictional Baker Street address where the detective lived. And Sherlock Holmes societies have proliferated throughout the world.

Conan Doyle sent the completed manuscript of *A Study in Scarlet* to James Payn, the editor who had already published some of his stories in the *Cornhill*. Payn returned it because it was too much like the ubiquitous "shilling shockers" already on the market. Furthermore, it was too long and would require an entire issue; and it was too short for single story. "It's too long—and too short—for the *Cornhill Magazine*," he wrote.

Doyle then sent the story to Arrowsmith in Bristol, who returned it after two months in pristine condition, apparently unread. Mailed in a cardboard cylinder, the rolled-up pages were not flattened out as they would have been had they been handled by editors. Frederick Warne & Company also rejected it.

Finally, acceptance came when Ward, Lock & Company offered him £25 for the rights, obviously not fully understanding what they had acquired. Also believing that the market was inundated with cheap fiction of this kind, they kept the story for a year. Nor did they assent to a fee based on royalties when Doyle made that request.

Not until December 1887 did the shocker appear in *Beeton's Christmas Annual*, which sold for a shilling. It went unnoticed, but when the edition sold out, Ward, Lock proposed a second. It was brought out in book form in 1888, but there was nothing in it for Doyle, who had sold the copyright. And it was pirated in America. Since international copyright laws were not established until 1891, it could be printed freely, and it was. The derisory payment of £25 was the total sum he realized for the novel that marks the debut of Sherlock Holmes.

The detective story was not the only genre that gave Conan Doyle difficulty. While waiting for *A Study in Scarlet* to be printed, he began a historical novel, *Micah Clarke*. Payn told him that the combination of fact and fiction was a waste. Blackwoods turned it down because the speech and the characters were not correct for the seventeenth century. Bentley found that it suffered from "a complete absence of interest." The Globe Newspaper Syndicate returned it because it had "no attraction for female readers" and "is hardly sensational enough." And Cassell's knew that historical novels were formulas for failures. Doyle made a final effort with Andrew Lang of Longmans Green, who accepted and published it in February 1889 to good critical reviews.

Doyle went on to write another work of historical fiction, *The White Company* (followed fourteen years later by *Sir Nigel*). He again approached Payn who, having realized his mistake on *Micah Clarke*, agreed this time to publish it in the *Cornhill*.

In America, the Philadelphia editor of *Lippincott's Monthly Magazine*, saw the potential of *A Study in Scarlet*. When he sailed to London in search of new talent and contributors for his publication, he arranged a dinner meeting with Conan Doyle. Also present at the meeting was Oscar Wilde. Wilde was signed to write *The Picture of Dorian Gray*, while Conan Doyle was commissioned to write another Sherlock Holmes story, *The Sign of the Four*. In that novel, as well as in a number of other Sherlock Holmes stories, appeared the site of the auspicious meeting, the Langham Hotel.

The Sign of the Four, issued in February 1890, set the pattern for Doyle's writing career. He may have wanted to produce historical fiction, but the public wanted his detective fiction. Specifically, the public wanted Sherlock Holmes.

While *Micah Clarke* went into second and third printings by Longmans Green, Sherlock Holmes was becoming an immortal character and a household name around the world. *The Strand Magazine* accepted the first Holmes short story ("A Scandal in Bohemia") and contracted for half a dozen more for £35 each. They proved to be tremendously successful, and the *Strand* wanted more. Doyle asked for and received £50. A demand for the fascinating detective was created. The fascination continues. Conan Doyle emerged triumphant and able to turn to writing for a living.

WILLIAM FAULKNER

".. . we don't believe that you should
offer it for publication. It is diffuse and
non-integral with neither very much plot
development nor character development.
... you don't seem to have any story to
tell and I contend that a novel should tell
a story and tell it well."

William Faulkner, one of the greatest of American literary
figures, was not immune to the sounds and furies signifying
rejection.

The Nobel prize-winning novelist, born in Mississippi on
25 September 1897, began his writing career as a poet. His
first published book, a slender volume of pastoral poems
entitled *The Marble Faun,* appeared in 1924 thanks to a
subsidy from a close friend. Phil Stone paid manufacturing
costs to the publisher, the Four Seas Company of Boston. It
was an unsuccessful volume that made few sales and had no
impact on the literary world. Faulkner was later to say, "I'm a
failed poet. Maybe every novelist wanted to write poetry first."
In any case, the second-rate poet turned to prose.

Although determined to be a writer, Faulkner held a
variety of odd jobs such as carpentering and housepainting to
earn money. In 1918 he spent five months in the RAF-Canada.
He worked in a New York City bookstore and as a postmaster

in his home town of Oxford, Mississippi, before traveling to New Orleans where he spent six important months in 1925. There he met Sherwood Anderson, who encouraged and influenced him greatly. He wrote pieces for *The Double Dealer*, and he contributed sixteen sketches to the *Times-Picayune* newspaper. That year he also completed his first novel, *Soldiers' Pay*, the major achievement of the New Orleans period. By recommending it to his own publisher, Sherwood Anderson was instrumental in the novel's immediate acceptance. Horace Liveright offered Faulkner a contract and an option on his next two works. *Soldiers' Pay*, about the homecoming of a dying soldier, appeared on 25 February 1926, published by Boni and Liveright.

Lillian Hellman was the reader assigned to Faulkner's next novel. She responded favorably, and on 30 April 1927, Boni and Liveright published his second novel, *Mosquitoes*, a satire on the role of art and artists in society. Conrad Aiken praised its style and wit before concluding that it was "good enough to make one wish that it were better."

With his third novel, Faulkner found his way. He felt more confident about this novel and enthusiastically informed his publisher in a letter in late July 1927 that it was "much better than that other stuff." When he completed it at the end of September, he told Liveright, "I have written THE book, of which those other things were but foals. I believe it is the damdest best book you'll look at this year, and any other publisher." Apparently his correspondent did not agree, for he rejected *Flags in the Dust*: "It is with sorrow in my heart that I write to tell you that three of us have read *Flags in the Dust* and don't believe Boni and Liveright should publish it. Furthermore," the letter continued, "as a firm deeply interested in your work, we don't believe that you should offer it for publication."

The publisher went on to cite the reasons for refusal: "It is diffuse and non-integral with neither very much plot development nor character development. We think it lacks plot, dimension and projection. The story really doesn't get anywhere and has a thousand loose ends. . . . My chief objection is that you don't seem to have any story to tell and I contend that a novel should tell a story and tell it well." On the grounds of lack of plot and structure, they dismissed any possibility of a revised and shortened version and returned the manuscript with the understanding that "you are to give us the refusal of your next book." The option included in Faulkner's contract placed the onus entirely on him. It obligated Faulkner to offer his next manuscript to the publisher, but the publisher was not obligated to accept it. So much for options!

Thus was Faulkner's elation squelched. Nevertheless, he continued to believe in the merits of *Flags in the Dust* and retained the hope that it would be "THE book" that would establish his credibility as an important writer. He responded to his editor, "It's too bad you dont like *Flags in the Dust*. . . I shall try it on someone else. I still believe it is the book which will make my name for me as a writer."

The rejected novel was in fact the one that established his mythical Yoknapatawpha County, a microcosm with subjects that rise to mythic proportions. It was the novel that initiated the long saga about the social history of Jefferson and the decadence of the Compson and Sartoris families, representatives of the Old South who are replaced by the unscrupulous Snopes clan. But the publisher saw it only as the novel with a story that "really doesn't get anywhere." He had not the vision to see that Faulkner had created characters and a cosmos, history and heredity, to which he would return in fourteen future novels including *The Sound and the Fury* (1929), *As I Lay Dying* (1930), *Sanctuary* (1931), *Light in*

August (1932), *Absolom, Absolom!* (1936), *The Hamlet* (1940), *Go Down, Moses* (1942), and *Requiem for a Nun* (1951).

At the start of 1928, stunned and disillusioned by the rejection, Faulkner nevertheless continued to hope that his third novel was marketable and submitted it to some dozen other publishers—only to receive numerous other refusals. (Accounts vary from eleven to eighteen.) Then he wearied of it and wanted nothing more to do with it. His friend and literary agent, Ben Wasson, managed to place it with Harcourt, Brace and Company, but with the stipulated condition that Wasson cut and edit the novel. Faulkner passively consented as it seemed the only means of seeing it in print. The new version involved more than substantial cutting. Transitions had to be inserted to bridge the gaps, and passages had to be rewritten before Harcourt published it as *Sartoris* in 1929.

While in the throes of trying to get his rebuffed novel to emerge in print, Faulkner began his fourth novel. He returned to a short story about Caddy Compson and expanded it to include her brothers. For the youngest of the four Compson children, he extracted the central character, an idiot tightly holding a broken narcissus, from an earlier story ("The Kingdom of God") written for a New Orleans newspaper. He transformed discouragement into creative release as the manuscript grew into his masterful *The Sound and the Fury*.

But Alfred Harcourt was not interested in the new manuscript and gave it to Harrison Smith, an editor who was leaving for partnership in a new firm, and added gratuitously, "You're the only damn fool in New York who would publish it." The house of Jonathan Cape and Harrison Smith—the new firm was his fourth publisher in little over four years—published *The Sound and the Fury* on 7 October 1929, the same year as *Sartoris*. According to one account by a former Cape and Smith reader, possibly exaggerated, a dozen

37

other publishers in addition to Harcourt had also refused *The Sound and the Fury*, the book that remains today simply one of the major novels of American literature.

The author of some of the most remarkable works of contemporary literature emerged from rejection and obscurity to achieve a position of eminence in the world. He produced altogether some twenty novels and over a hundred short stories, as well as poems, plays, essays, speeches, and Hollywood film scripts—an impressive and massive array. In 1950 he was awarded the Nobel Prize for literature. A dozen years later, appeared his last novel, *The Reivers*, on 4 June. Just one month afterwards, on 6 July 1962, Faulkner died of a heart attack. *Flags in the Dust*, the original and rejected version of *Sartoris*, was reconstructed for posthumous publication in 1973.

F. SCOTT FITZGERALD

".. .we cannot offer to publish it as it
stands at present. . . .we should welcome
a chance to reconsider its publication."

As a young man in St. Paul, Minnesota, where he was born on
24 September 1896, F. Scott Fitzgerald showed enormous
potential as an apprentice writer. His first story appeared in
the school magazine in 1909. In 1911 he was sent to the
Newman Academy in Hackensack, New Jersey. Its proximity
to New York enabled him to attend theatre in the city and to
connect his early literary ambitions with the stage. However,
the plays he later wrote were unsuccessful. At Princeton, he
suffered from ill health and poor grades and withdrew to
accept a commission in the army as second lieutenant.

The young army officer and aspiring writer from
Minnesota entrusted a novel he had written in the spring of
1918 to his friend and mentor Shane Leslie. Leslie sent the
manuscript that was at first called *The Romantic Egotist* to
Charles Scribner, where it made the rounds of editors. One
editor "could not stomach it at all." Another found it "hard
sledding." And Maxwell Perkins, that genius of an editor who
discovered so many young talents, commended its vitality and
originality but went on with his courteous letter of reluctant
rejection citing unavailability of paper, high manufacturing
costs, and "certain characteristics of the novel itself."

Perkins liked F. Scott Fitzgerald's novel despite the flaws. He criticized it but at the same time recognized its power. "The protagonist," he wrote, "leaves the reader distinctly disappointed and dissatisfied." He made comments and suggestions for revising the manuscript, a practice he seldom indulged in, and held out the hope that after revision "we should welcome a chance to reconsider its publication."

Lieutenant Fitzgerald quickly rewrote his novel in six weeks and sent it off by mid-October. But he was too distracted and impatient to do the thorough revision that was needed. Perkins found it much improved, but the older editors again voted against acceptance. Believing in its merits, Perkins showed the book to two rival publishers. But they also rebuffed it. Fitzgerald lost interest when the book was turned down a second time. He had met and fallen in love with Zelda Sayre while he was stationed near Montgomery, Alabama, and needed now to achieve financial independence and security in order to win her. He took a job as a copywriter in an advertising agency and wrote stories in the evenings, most of which were returned.

The year was 1919 and he was a failure. His engagement to Zelda Sayre was broken, he was working in an advertising agency, his stories were being returned, and his novel had been rejected. He decided to return to his parents' home in St. Paul where he could cloister himself in his old room on the third floor and devote himself to perfecting his novel. He finished *The Education of a Personage* that summer and contacted Perkins about it. In September he was able to submit his completely revised manuscript with its new title, *This Side of Paradise*.

The editorial battle was heated. Mr. Scribner declined the book that had no "literary merit" while Brownell called it "frivolous." Perkins presented an argument that was tantamount to a resignation: "My feeling is that a publisher's first allegiance is to talent. And if we aren't going to publish a talent like this, it is a very serious thing. . . . If we're going to turn down the likes of Fitzgerald, I will lose all interest in publishing books." If publication were refused, he concluded, "we might as well go out of business." As a result of his forceful argument, the manuscript which he believed "abounds in energy and life" was accepted. Perkins supported Fitzgerald for the rest of his life. And Fitzgerald needed support.

A week after publication of *This Side of Paradise* on 26 March 1920, on the strength of his first novel, he married Zelda Sayre, whose developing schizophrenia would plague his marriage. But for the present, his brief apprenticeship was over and he was at a peak of happiness. By April his first novel was in a second printing. It was an overwhelming success and made him a celebrity at twenty-four. Although his experience in the world of rejection slips was relatively short lived, his was not a case of instant acceptance. But when acceptance did come, it was colossal. Fitzgerald's career had apparently taken off, and it seemed the dawn of a new and successful destiny. It was his hope that he could now support himself by continuing to produce best-selling novels.

But he succumbed to potboiler stories to pay the bills. He had written stories for magazines while awaiting publication of his first novel, many of which were declined, and submitted eleven more within a month of publication of his novel. Magazines wanted only optimistic and enjoyable stories, and he created a dream world of jazz and dancing, full of smoking, drinking, and extravagant spending. He and Zelda lived lavishly and came to be accepted as the quintessential Jazz Age couple.

Fitzgerald's best magazine stories, written from 1919 to 1925, from *This Side of Paradise* to *The Great Gatsby*, were collected and published in three volumes: *Flappers and*

Philosophers (1920), *Tales of the Jazz Age* (1922), and *All the Sad Young Men* (1926).

His second novel, *The Beautiful and Damned* was published on 3 March 1922 and *The Great Gatsby,* considered to be his finest novel, on 10 April 1925. *The Great Gatsby* was a great critical success, hailed by T. S. Eliot as "the first step that American fiction has taken since Henry James."

But for Fitzgerald, who had written it at twenty-eight and published seven books between 1920 and 1926, *The Great Gatsby* was not enough of a commercial success. There seemed never to be enough money to satisfy the extravagant life style of the Fitzgeralds. *The Vegetable,* a satirical play that failed in 1923, sent him further into debt. He could not meet expenses and returned to writing popular and lucrative rubbish. He was unable to settle down to becoming a serious novelist. Indeed, he seemed bent on self-destruction and made little progress after the publication of *Gatsby.* In late summer of 1925 he began his next book, which would materialize some eight years later, after five starts and seventeen versions, as *Tender Is the Night.*

The 1930s represents a decade of decline and dissolution with continuing deterioration of Zelda's mental state, his alcoholism and poor health, and uncontrollable debts. The long-awaited *Tender Is the Night* appeared on 12 April 1934, an ambitious novel in which he examined the decline of the protagonist, perhaps trying to understand Zelda's mental breakdown and his share of responsibility in it. He also began in 1935 his three "Crack-Up" essays which broke ground for later writers who opened up about their personal anguish. He became a Hollywood script writer. *The Last Tycoon,* his last novel, was left unfinished and published posthumously when he died of a heart attack on 21 December 1940, at the age of forty-four.

JOHN GALSWORTHY

An editor softened the blow of rejection
with kind words: "I think however you
will soon find a publisher .... It is too good
to be passed over for long."

John Galsworthy trained for a career in law but was obsessed
with the idea of writing. Born in 1867, he was educated
at Harrow and Oxford and qualified as a barrister; but
he remained singularly unenthusiastic about the legal
profession. The vocation he wanted was not the one his
lawyer-father had pressed on him.

Galsworthy first appeared in print in 1897 under the
pseudonym of John Sinjohn. *From the Four Winds,* a collection
of short stories, was published by special arrangement with
Fisher Unwin. The author would pay for the printing while the
publisher would receive a commission based on the number
of copies sold, thus insuring that the publisher had nothing
whatever to lose even if the book turned out to be an utter
failure. (Nevertheless, despite such inequitable terms, I
suspect that many of today's aspiring writers with means
would snatch at such a contract in order to fulfill the
cherished wish to become an author.)

The book was indeed an utter failure. Five hundred copies
were printed, but the edition did not sell out. And Galsworthy,
rather ashamed of his first effort, never allowed a reprinting.

He even referred to his first book in the Nobel Prize Address of 1932 as "that dreadful little book." Fortunately, he also recognized its importance to his career as a writer and refused to submit to such unfavorable terms in his subsequent efforts. The following year, on 29 January 1898, he sent the manuscript of his next work, *Jocelyn*, again to Fisher Unwin, who promptly rejected it, simply unwilling to take any risk. With somewhat more foresight, Gerald Duckworth took it on. There followed two more novels by John Sinjohn, *Villa Rubein* (1900) and *A Man of Devon* (1901), before Galsworthy came out of the closet and abandoned his assumed name.

He established a pattern of a novel every year or two, but *The Island Pharisees* did not appear until 1904, due to the rewriting suggested by Edward Garnett, a mentor and member of his circle of literary friends that included also the illustrious Joseph Conrad. Conrad had offered an earlier version of *The Island Pharisees* to Hallam Murray; when they declined, he wrote to Galsworthy, "they are beasts . . . No work is judged on its artistic merits."

Edward Garnett, the critic and writer of essays and plays, was a reader to Duckworth & Company. But the failure of *Jocelyn* and *Villa Rubein* caused the firm to reject Galsworthy's fifth book in spite of Garnett's strong recommendation. In a supportive letter of 20 May 1903, Garnett softened the blow of rejection with words of confidence: "I think however you will soon find a publisher if you stick to *The Pharisees*. It is too good to be passed over for long, though we must expect temporary rebuffs." After another rebuff from Constable, Edward Garnett took it to Pawling of Heinemann, who, with great insight or luck or both, accepted it on condition that Galsworthy offer his next book to the firm.

His next book was simply his most famous novel, *The Man of Property*. His first financially successful novel—it was reissued four times between 1906 and 1911—marked the opening of his epic *Forsyte Saga*, while the year 1906 marked the peak of his career.

He also produced his well-received first play, *The Silver Box*, which made him the most popular new playwright of 1906. It was followed by *The Country House* in 1907 and by a long string of successful writings in both genres, all to high acclaim.

So much for the chronological beginning of a writing span of over thirty-five years, a career that produced altogether twenty novels, twenty-seven plays, and nearly twenty volumes of collected pieces including poems.

When *The Man of Property* together with *In Chancery* (1920) and *To Let* (1921) came out in 1922 as a trilogy, Galsworthy, at fifty-five, became world famous. His last six novels formed the second and third of the vast and vastly popular trilogies.

Awards and honors piled up. He refused a knighthood on the grounds that men of letters who write philosophy and criticism of life should not accept titles. But he accepted the Order of Merit. He was awarded honorary degrees from over half a dozen universities. And near the end of his life, he received the Nobel Prize for literature. Too ill to attend the award ceremony in 1932, he died in January 1933.

Perhaps the greatest tribute came in 1967, the centenary year of his birth, when the BBC created a resurgence of interest in Galsworthy by producing a lengthy television serialization of *The Forsyte Chronicles*. The twenty-six episode dramatization, seen by millions the world over, was repeated by popular demand the following year.

John Galsworthy remains one of the leading authors of the century, and Heinemann, which continued to publish his novels, has always kept the Forsyte trilogies in print. His popularity has led to the reissue of *Beyond, The Country House, The Dark Flower, Fraternity, The Island Pharisees,*

Saint's Progress, and so on. Even his rejected novel, *Jocelyn,* was reissued in 1976.

A final word on his current status might be measured by his very first rejected book, *From the Four Winds.* While the exact value today may be difficult to estimate, an original copy sold for $1000 in New York in 1929. Who would know the name of Galsworthy today if he had relinquished his obsession to write and returned to a career in law?

GEORGE GISSING

"It possesses a great deal of graphic
power and some humour, but in our
opinion it is very deficient in dramatic
interest. . . .it fails to meet the
requirements of the reader of fiction."

During a writing career of twenty-three years, George Gissing
produced twenty-one novels, one hundred eleven short
stories, a travel book, a number of essays, and a critical study
that continues to be regarded as one of the best ever written
on Dickens. A leading novelist of the 1890s, he had to his
credit at least four titles which will continue to keep his
reputation alive: *Demos* (1886), *New Grub Street* (1891), *Born
in Exile* (1892), and *The Odd Women* (1893). A recent revival of
interest has resulted in new editions of the novels of George
Gissing.

That Gissing's life as a young man reads like one of his
own novels may be due to his use of particular incidents and
segments of his own existence in his writings. Briefly, he
became involved with a young Manchester girl of the streets,
was dismissed from Owens College (later to be the University
of Manchester) when he stole from the common room to
meet her demands, spent a month in jail, and went in disgrace
to America. On his return to England, he married and tried
to redeem the girl whose alcoholism, irresponsibility,

47

slovenliness, and occasional return to ply her old trade, made her simply irredeemable; he eventually separated from her.

It was in America that he first tried to earn a living as a writer. His first published work was a critical essay in the Boston *Commonwealth* on two paintings exhibited in Boston. Apparently happily employed as a high school teacher in suburban Waltham, he left suddenly and inexplicably for Chicago, where his career as a writer of fiction began with an autobiographical short story for the Chicago *Tribune* called "The Sins of the Fathers." It was followed by "R.I.P." and other stories for other papers, at least seventeen of which were published between March and July 1877. Soon thereafter, the starving and homesick Gissing borrowed enough money for the return passage to England.

Back in London in 1877, he continued to live in poverty, tutoring and writing in his spare time, but feeling unsuited to a career in journalism. He finished a novel and sent it to at least one publisher. He reported its lack of success in a letter of July 1878 to his brother: "The publishers respectfully decline the honour of publishing my novel." Nothing is known of this untitled and forgotten novel which no one wanted and which has not survived, but he immediately started another, completing it in about a year.

The new novel, *Workers in the Dawn*, was also rejected by a succession of publishing firms. In November 1879, Chatto & Windus gave him false hope by keeping the novel for an inordinately long time. When they eventually returned the manuscript expressing polite regret, Gissing sent it to Messrs. Smith Elder & Co.

Smith Elder also declined: "It possesses a great deal of graphic power and some humour, but in our opinion it is very deficient in dramatic interest. As a series of scenes the book is good, but as a continued tale it fails to meet the requirements of the reader of fiction."

Sampson, Low & Company declined although they found it to be "undoubtedly very ably written, that is our reader's opinion; but we are sorry to say he does not recommend it to us, on account of its rationalistic tendency, and certain details of a profligate character. We do not believe in fiction being the proper vehicle for conveying doctrinal opinions, for one reason that most readers will not read them."

Pouncing on the view that it was "ably written" and bent on publication, he sent it to C. Kegan Paul who promised "an early and careful consideration." Then they too declined. Undiscouraged, he did two things. He provided the basis for publication. And he wrote another.

"At last!—I have obtained a publisher for my novel." So wrote an exhilarated Gissing to his brother in February 1880. "The publishers are Messrs. Remington & Co." he continued. "Only let the book see the light of day, as I was determined it should." In actual fact, his determination was so great that he had arranged to publish it at his own expense.

Gissing had received on his twenty-first birthday, 22 November 1878, a legacy of about £500 left by his father. He was able to pay off the debt he had incurred in America and use the balance to pay for production of his first novel. The contract with Remington and Company called for the sum of £125 to cover 277 copies of the three-volume set of *Workers in the Dawn*. The author would receive two thirds of the profits after advertising expenses were deducted. Thus was Gissing's first novel published in 1880 when he was only twenty-two years of age.

After the first three months, he complained that advertising was inadequate. Only forty-nine copies had been sold; and he could justifiably doubt the firm's honesty when he earned altogether, for the first year's sale, sixteen shillings. Gissing was a victim of the common practice designed to eliminate risk to the publisher. He was never to earn much money from his writing, and his life remained a constant struggle to make ends meet.

Nevertheless, having embraced a career as an author, he went on writing and completed *Mrs. Grundy's Enemies* in September 1882. It underwent the usual round of rejections with Smith Elder returning it as "too painful" to attract subscribers to Mudie's lending library. Bentley and Company accepted it in December 1882 for a token payment of fifty pounds. But Gissing was delighted that at least it would be published.

He was soon to learn what others in the trade already knew: Bentley was a scoundrel. While the manuscript was in proof, the publisher asked for changes of certain objectionable scenes. Gissing gave way. Bentley requested further excisions, and Gissing again complied. Despite further revisions, he was still awaiting publication in February 1884. But the novel was never published, and both manuscript and proofs have been lost.

The Unclassed, completed toward the end of 1883, was rejected by George Bentley because sympathetic portrayal of a prostitute might lead the young to go astray. The subject was not "wholesome" and dealt with "things best not dwelt upon." Bentley concluded that "it is not from want of talent that I feel obliged to decline your book, but the nature of the story itself." The reader for Chapman & Hall, George Meredith, suggested changes for *The Unclassed,* and Gissing revised. He was paid a paltry thirty pounds, and his second published novel appeared in the middle of June 1884.

Not until *Demos*, his third published and first great novel, was "the awful decade"—as he called the years 1876 to 1885—over. With *Demos* he emerged from obscurity to become a major Victorian novelist. But his income remained modest, and he continued to endure publishing difficulties.

With *Demos*, he should have been published happily ever after. But he had trouble placing his next novel. The parsimony of publishers might be understood with an author whose books do not sell, but *Demos* did sell and should have given him a bargaining advantage for future novels. Not a good negotiator, Gissing tended to prefer outright sale of copyright for instant relief of his impecunious circumstances. Moreover, he reasoned, as publishers were under no obligation to show their accounts, authors could be cheated in a royalty agreement.

Although he was now an established novelist, Gissing did not benefit from his recognized position. When Smith Elder offered a mere fifty pounds for *Thyrza*, he rationalized, "to hunt for a new publisher would be to ruin the rest of the year's work. . . . No, I must take their offer." He also accepted their offers of £150 for the copyright of *The Nether World* (1889) and £150 for *New Grub Street* (1891). *New Grub Street* went into a second edition just seven weeks after publication, followed by five cheap editions in England as well as publication in foreign countries. The author received only the benefit of popularity and demand for more fiction. Naturally, the pitiless publisher was unwilling to adjust the terms of the contract.

Gissing sent *Born in Exile* to James Payn of Smith Elder asking for a £250 payment. Payn was about to leave on holiday and would not even consider reading it before at least a month's time. Nor would he pay the amount asked. Intimidated, Gissing countered with a lower figure of £150 if only he could be given immediate payment, whereupon Payn returned the manuscript unread, adding gratuitously that his books were too lugubrious to sell.

Gissing next hired an agent who obtained an offer from Chatto and Windus of £120, an amount that fell under the set minimum goal of £200. Then Longmans rejected it. And Bentley. (That he would return to Bentley after the appalling treatment meted out to him testifies in part to his desperation.) *Born in Exile* went finally to Adam and Charles Black for a mere £100 after deduction of the agent's ten per cent commission and appeared in May 1892.

A brighter publishing light shone when the new firm of Lawrence and Bullen approached Gissing and offered to produce his new novel, *Denzil Quarrier,* in a six-shilling format, giving him one shilling on every copy sold plus a £100 advance. It was the start of a long and pleasant association. Eager to have his work, they shared profits with him and treated him fairly. To Lawrence and Bullen he sent *The Odd Women,* his 1893 novel on the problem of social status of women. It continues to be popular today, particularly in the feminist movement, and continues to be reprinted.

One measure of the success he managed to achieve came in January 1895 in the form of a surprising request for a novel from Smith Elder, the publisher who had previously rejected *Born in Exile* unread. Another measure of his literary success came with the last and most successful book of his lifetime, *The Private Papers of Henry Ryecroft* (1903). Praised by reviewers as a spiritual autobiography and a masterpiece, it went through four editions before George Gissing died on 28 December 1903.

Despite his ongoing battle with publishers, Gissing has won a high place in literary history; an abiding interest in his works insures his reputation as a major novelist.

THOMAS HARDY

"... of far too sensational an order for us
to think of publishing."

Like many aspiring authors, Thomas Hardy's early road to
fame and success was a difficult one. Like many, he began in
an entirely unrelated career. He was born on 2 June 1840 in
a small thatched cottage three miles from the county town
of Dorchester in Dorset—the epicenter of the Wessex
countryside that he was later to develop in his fiction. His
birthplace in Upper Bockhampton was to become a shrine
receiving vast numbers of visitors who arrive at the cottage,
now owned by the National Trust and open to the public, to
pay homage to the great novelist and poet.

Hardy trained initially as an architect. When his schooling
came to an end in the summer of 1856, shortly after his
sixteenth birthday, he was apprenticed for three years to a
Dorchester architect who specialized in the restoration of
Gothic churches. Afterwards he departed for London for
employment as an architectural assistant. The big city offered
also an opportunity to pursue another ambition, and he began
a literary apprenticeship. When his youthful poems failed to
find a publisher, he turned to fiction in hopes of achieving a
greater success. His first published piece, a sketch entitled
"How I Built Myself a House," appeared on 18 March 1865 in
Chambers's Journal.

Ill health precipitated his return to Dorset in July 1867, where he resumed his work as an architectural assistant on a freelance basis while writing in his spare time. By the end of the year he completed the first draft of his first novel, *The Poor Man and the Lady*, a satire on the upper classes. He was an unknown writer of twenty-eight when he sent the manuscript to Macmillan in July 1868. Before the end of the year, Alexander Macmillan wrote a thoughtful letter pointing out the strengths as well as the flaws of the novel that he read "with much interest and admiration" but declining to publish the novel that contained "fatal drawbacks to its success. . . ." He concluded with encouraging words: "I am writing to you as to a writer. . . at least potentially. . . of power & purpose. If this is your first book I think you ought to go on."

Hardy did go on. He revised the manuscript, removing the offending passages, and submitted it again to Macmillan in late November. In December, Macmillan confirmed the rejection but gave Hardy an introduction to Chapman and Hall. Frederick Chapman accepted it on condition that Hardy pay a guarantee of twenty pounds against losses. Hardy agreed. Before the contract arrived, however, he was summoned to London for an interview with George Meredith, the publisher's reader, who expressed concern that publication might elicit savage attacks by reviewers and be detrimental to future prospects. Although the firm was still willing to publish it, he suggested sweeping changes. In fact, he suggested sweeping it away and beginning again.

Hardy returned to Dorset with the failed manuscript to nurse his dejection and consider his options. He made another attempt, sending it to Smith Elder in April. Their prompt rejection arrived in two weeks. He decided to try just one more publisher and submitted it to Tinsley Brothers in June. They kept it for three months before making an offer. But William Tinsley's terms for publication involved a greater payment than Hardy could afford, and the would-be author had to refuse. He had to abandon hope and admit that the novel was unacceptable, that he had lost the two-year struggle for publication. Hardy adapted parts of it in later works, but the novel was never issued and has not survived. Hardy always remembered the bitterness of rejection of this unpublishable novel.

In Dorset, as an architectural assistant, he undertook church restoration work in Weymouth and began another novel using that town (Budmouth in his fiction) as a setting for *Desperate Remedies*. He was able to send the new manuscript (which contained extracted parts of his failed novel) to Alexander Macmillan on 5 March 1870, just before leaving to work on the St. Juliot Rectory in Cornwall, where he was to meet his future wife. A month later came the report from John Morley praising certain aspects but condemning it for "the disgusting and absurd outrage which is the key to its mystery. The violation of a young girl at an evening party, and the subsequent birth of a child, is too abominable to be tolerated as a central incident from which the action of the story is to move." Macmillan rejected it on 5 April despite "very decided qualities, & very considerable power" because it was "of far too sensational an order for us to think of publishing."

He overlooked Chapman and Hall this time and sent it off immediately to Tinsley, who again offered to publish it, again on condition of payment of a subsidy. Hardy would be required to make some revisions and apply £75 as a guarantee against any losses incurred. Hardy, indeed the poor man of his first novel, had only £123 to his name, but this time he did not refuse Tinsley's terms, and his first published novel appeared on 25 March 1871, anonymously, in three volumes. It was the start of a literary career that lasted for fifty-seven years. Hardy was in later life to recall the elated, victorious feelings he experienced: "Never will I forget the thrill that ran through me from head to foot when I held my first copy of *Desperate Remedies* in my hand."

Of 500 copies printed, 370 were sold; the author lost a third of his money. But he was finally a published author and, despite the inferior nature of his debut novel, was launched in a career as a struggling novelist rather than a struggling architect. He wrote novels and short stories for the next twenty-five years. And after his position in the literary world was secure, he turned back to poetry, which he wrote until his death on 11 January 1928 in his eighty-eighth year.

Meanwhile, with his usual determination, he began another novel, *Under the Greenwood Tree,* and again sent the manuscript off to Macmillan on 7 August 1871. A letter from Alexander Macmillan dated 18 October 1871 expresses the fear that "the public will find the tale very slight and unexciting. The first 50 or 60 pages too are really rather tedious and should be shortened by about one half." Unwilling to take a risk, the publisher continued with ambiguous words of rejection: "We could not venture it now, as our hands are full of Christmas books; besides it is hardly a good time for 'Under the Greenwood Tree.' But if you should not arrange otherwise before the Spring I should like to have the opportunity of deciding as to whether we could do it for an early summer or Spring book. I return the MS." Hardy arranged otherwise. He went to Tinsley, who paid £30 for the copyright. (He was to sell it back later for £300.) *Under the Greenwood Tree* appeared, again anonymously, in June 1872.

Macmillan simply lacked gambling instinct, unlike Tinsley who asked for and received a serial story to begin in the September issue of *Tinsley's Magazine,* his popular monthly publication. *A Pair of Blue Eyes,* Hardy's novel with a Cornish setting, came out first in serial form and in volume form in May 1873. The last in the trio of first-published novels marks also his last apprentice piece.

Hardy's name came to the attention of Sir Leslie Stephen, the well-known critic and editor of the *Dictionary of National Biography* and father of Virginia Woolf. Stephen admired *Under the Greenwood Tree* sufficiently to request a story for the prestigious *Cornhill Magazine*, of which he was the editor. Hardy complied with *Far from the Madding Crowd.* The twelve-part serialization began in the January 1874 issue and made Hardy famous. In November, Smith Elder (publishers of the *Cornhill*) brought out a two-volume edition of *Far from the Madding Crowd,* one of Hardy's six major novels, and the one in which he first gave the old Saxon name of Wessex to his geographical region. Hardy was in demand, and the *Cornhill* wanted another story. He was on the way to achieving a respected and permanent place in literary history.

His novels continued to emerge first as serials before being issued in book form. The practice of serialization, widely used in the nineteenth century by such writers as Charles Dickens and Wilkie Collins, guaranteed a large audience. Moreover, as with today's film versions, magazine serials stimulated book sales.

As an established novelist, Hardy experienced only minor publishing difficulties as he went on to produce major novels: *The Return of the Native* (1878), *The Mayor of Casterbridge* (1886), *The Woodlanders* (1887), *Tess of the D'Urbervilles* (1891), and *Jude the Obscure* (1895). A total of altogether fourteen novels, over forty short stories, and 947 poems has insured a respected and enduring reputation.

ERNEST HEMINGWAY

"It would be in extremely rotten taste, to
say nothing of being horribly cruel,
should we have wanted to publish it . . . .
we are rejecting *Torrents of Spring*
because we disagree with you. . . that it
is a fine and humorous American satire."

More astonishing than the fact of Hemingway's early rejection
is the truly astonishing possibility that he engineered his own
rejection.

Hemingway had settled in Paris after the First World War
and was earning a living as a news correspondent before he
became the leading spokesman for the "lost generation." He
was also writing stories and poems. His first published book,
a slim volume with the descriptive title of *Three Stories and
Ten Poems* appeared in 1923.

In 1924 a collection of his short stories was published
in Paris under the title *in our time*. In America, George Doran
was first to turn it down believing short stories to be
commercially unviable. Maxwell Perkins of Charles
Scribner's Sons, the New York editor famous for discovering
gifted young writers, was "greatly impressed by the power in
the scenes and incidents pictured" but regretted declining the
slender book for economic reasons: "it is so small that it would
give the booksellers no opportunity for substantial profit if

issued at a price which custom would dictate." However, Perkins wanted to consider whatever Hemingway was writing.

Hemingway managed to sell the book of vignettes centering on the life of Nick Adams to Boni and Liveright, who published *In Our Time* (now capitalized) in October 1924. The contract signed on 31 March gave the publisher an option on his next three books. Shortly after Hemingway signed the contract, Maxwell Perkins contacted him because a leading young author of his, F. Scott Fitzgerald, had persuaded him that Hemingway was a brilliant writer with a vast potential who ought to be recruited for Scribners. The letter had been delayed and arrived too late to acquire Hemingway, who admitted that he would more happily have joined Scribners and would gladly submit another book to Perkins if the contract he had lately signed should ever lapse.

When, in the summer of 1925, Hemingway completed a first draft of *The Sun Also Rises*, he set aside his manuscript for a few weeks before coming back for a rewrite. Meanwhile, he spent a week writing *The Torrents of Spring*, which he submitted to Boni and Liveright. Although the firm's three-book option would become invalid if they declined any further submissions, Boni and Liveright declined *The Torrents of Spring*. The book was a 28,000-word merciless parody of Sherwood Anderson, an attack on his literary style. How could they possibly risk insulting one of their most important authors whose most recent work, *Dark Laughter*, was in its tenth printing? Horace Liveright had little alternative but to cable Hemingway: "Rejecting Torrents of spring/ Patiently awaiting ms sun also rises/ Writing fully"

He followed up the cable, writing fully a long letter dated 30 December 1925 which asked, "who on earth do you think would buy it? Entirely apart from the fact that it is such a bitter, and I might say almost vicious caricature of Sherwood

Anderson, it is so entirely cerebral." He concluded that "it would be in extremely rotten taste, to say nothing of being horribly cruel, should we have wanted to publish it. . . .So you must understand that we are rejecting *Torrents of Spring* because we disagree with you . . . that it is a fine and humorous American satire." But by turning it down, Liveright released Hemingway from the terms of the contract. He would not receive the promised book, *The Sun Also Rises*, the novel which was to establish Hemingway as a major literary figure.

There are those who maintain that Hemingway wrote the book as a contract breaker and that his submission was a clever ruse to extricate himself from obligation to Boni and Liveright. He had grievances against the publisher for improper handling of *In Our Time*. Sales were poor, he maintained, because the jacket was inappropriate and advertising was insufficient. Nor was it adequately appreciated by Liveright, who had insisted on deletion of the story about a dockside seduction, "Up in Michigan."

Hemingway also had grievances against his friend Sherwood Anderson, whom he had first met in Chicago in 1921. At that time, he was impressed with the established writer and influenced by his stories. Anderson befriended and encouraged the young apprentice and helped him get *In Our Time* published and praised. But Hemingway now felt that *Dark Laughter* was pretentious, sentimental, and insincere. Furthermore, he resented comparisons that reviewers inevitably made between Anderson's *Winesburg, Ohio* and his own first book of stories. He needed to dissociate himself, to announce his literary independence. Although Hemingway always denied that he contrived the scheme, a case can be made that *The Torrents of Spring* was a device for venting his objections and breaking with the publisher.

Fitzgerald, who had persisted in his praise of Hemingway, continued to badger Perkins and persuaded him to accept both *Torrents of Spring* and *The Sun Also Rises*, sight unseen. Torrents of Scribner books followed: *Men Without Women* (1927), *A Farewell to Arms* (1929), *Death in the Afternoon* (1932), *Winner Take Nothing* (1933), *Green Hills of Africa* (1935), *To Have and Have Not* (1937), *For Whom the Bell Tolls* (1940), *Across the River and into the Trees* (1950), and *The Old Man and the Sea* (1952). The long list culminated in a Nobel Prize for literature in 1954, before the bells tolled for Hemingway with his death by suicide in 1961, at the age of sixty-two.

A. E. HOUSMAN

Not recognizing its future or its merits,
the publishing establishment refused
Housman's famous first volume of
poetry.

A. E. Housman's reputation as a poet is based largely on his
first volume of verse, *A Shropshire Lad*. The collection of short
lyrics is so well known that most people are familiar at least
with the title of the book.

Yet the famous book was rebuffed by publishers. After
Macmillan turned it down, promptly and apparently without
comment, Housman asked his old Oxford friend and fellow
classics scholar at Oxford, Alfred Pollard, to read the
manuscript. He was cheered by Pollard's excitement over the
poems and his judgment that they would still be read in two
hundred years.

Pollard made two suggestions which helped to secure
publication: first, that he change the unpromising title of
Poems by Terence Hearsay to the more salubrious and
evocative *A Shropshire Lad*; and second, that he take the
manuscript to the publishing firm of Kegan Paul.

A Shropshire Lad was indeed published by Kegan Paul. An
agreement was reached and an edition of five hundred copies
was issued in 1896–but at the poet's own expense. The firm
provided its name, but Housman provided the money, making

full payment of thirty pounds in advance. (The arrangement was a common practice of the time for little books of verse.) That year, the highly-praised *A Shropshire Lad* sold only 381 copies. Two years after publication six copies remained unsold and warranted a second edition although the publisher had done little to stimulate sales.

Grant Richards was among those who had reviewed the book favorably. His enthusiasm remained vital when he formed his own small publishing company shortly thereafter, and he approached Housman for permission to take over the rights. Housman was amenable, and Richards published an edition of five hundred copies at his own expense and risk in September 1898.

Housman refused to take a royalty or any share of the profits saying, "I am a professor of Latin. I do not wish to make profit out of my poetry." Perhaps he felt it ludicrous to accept money now for the book whose publication he had to pay for originally. Or possibly he wished to conceal his concern for its success by a facade of unconcern over profits.

Richards remained his publisher and continued to bring out new editions. A third printing of one thousand copies in March 1900 was half sold by the end of the year, and another two thousand copies emerged from the press at the end of 1902.

It was a slow and steady climb for *A Shropshire Lad* to establish Housman's reputation and bring fame and immortality to the poet. He had come a long way since his first publication when he was a Worcestershire lad of fifteen and won the Bromsgrove School prize for his verse composition, "The Death of Socrates." Although he had not even submitted the poem, it won also the distinction of appearing in the local newspaper, the Bromsgrove *Messenger*.

At Oxford, he had again made several literary contributions to the undergraduate magazine. But he failed the exams and afterwards moved to London, taking a post at the Patent Office which he kept for ten years. In his spare time, he studied Greek and Latin at the British Museum Library and became a leading classics scholar. At this time, came the first of his scholarly publications in *The Journal of Philology*. His ongoing contributions to academic journals led to his appointment as Professor of Latin at University College, London, in 1892 and as Professor of Latin at Cambridge in 1911. Altogether he published well over a hundred reviews or articles on Greek and Latin subjects and critical editions of Manilus, Juvenal, and Lucan.

When *A Shropshire Lad* eventually caught on, the public and the publisher clamored for more poems. But Housman, immersed in Latin scholarship and professorial duties at Cambridge, took twenty-five years before releasing *Last Poems* when he was sixty-three. It was a huge success when it finally appeared in 1922 in a large edition of 4000. His poetry output may have been small, but it was extraordinary.

And when he was seventy-seven, on 30 April 1936, death came for the great poet-scholar who will always be remembered for the volume that would have been forgotten if the publishers had their way, *A Shropshire Lad*.

JAMES JOYCE

*". . . too discursive, formless,
unrestrained. . . ugly words are too
prominent."*

If there is something more painful than rejection of a manuscript it must surely be acceptance of a manuscript—followed
by retraction and rejection. That is what happened to James
Joyce with his first important work, his only book of short
stories, *Dubliners.* Twice.

But he learned about rejection much earlier in life. In
1900, when he was eighteen and considering the study of
medicine, Joyce wrote a play about a doctor called *A Brilliant
Career* that he sent to William Archer. The publisher was
impressed enough to send an encouraging personal reply but
not impressed enough to publish the play that has not
survived. Joyce tried William Archer again in 1901 with poems
and again received a personal reply but not acceptance.

His collection of poems called *Chamber Music* appeared
when he was twenty-five. But first it underwent the usual
round of rejections. The English publisher Grant Richards
lost the manuscript and requested a second copy, only to turn
it down in May 1905. Then, John Lane (who was to publish
Ulysses thirty years later) turned it down in June, Heinemann
in July, and Constable in October. Finally, Elkin Mathews
published *Chamber Music* early in May 1907.

65

In February 1906, Grant Richards accepted *Dubliners*. However, the book contained objectionable material such as the use of the word "bloody" and references to the royal family. Arguments ensued about alterations and deletions. Joyce, insisting on artistic integrity, refused to make substantial changes, and Richards became increasingly anxious about possible criminal prosecution. After almost a year of dickering and bickering, Grant Richards withdrew his offer, and the search for a publisher resumed.

John Long's rejection in February 1907 caused dejection. Elkin Mathews' decision to refuse *Dubliners* the following November was probably influenced by poor sales of *Chamber Music*. Hutchinson & Company refused even to look at the manuscript. Alston River turned it down in February 1908 and Edward Arnold, in July. Having failed to find an English publisher, Joyce sent *Dubliners* to the Dublin firm of Maunsel & Company the following year and achieved an acceptance that was again frustrated.

The second fiasco over *Dubliners* was even more painful because the book was actually printed, then destroyed. This time, Joyce signed a contract with George Roberts, managing director of the firm, to publish *Dubliners* in December 1909. Roberts kept delaying on various pretexts, and the argument lasted until 1912. Joyce eventually had to agree to eliminate all potentially libelous material as well as one entire story; but he insisted on a disclaimer in the book informing the reader that essential parts were missing. The publisher continued to mislead until finally he refused publication altogether. And the printer (who was also subject to criminal prosecution in English law) burned the entire edition of one thousand copies, refusing even to sell the printed sheets to Joyce. Seven years had elapsed since Joyce first approached Richards, but still *Dubliners* remained unpublished.

Dubliners continued to have bad luck. In London, Mr. Boon of Mills and Boon turned it down. Martin & Secker had the chance to consider *Dubliners* in December 1912 but became another name on the list of those who refused it. In February 1913 Joyce wrote to Elkin Mathews, publishers of *Chamber Music*, offering *Dubliners* at his own expense. Mathews turned him down twice, writing on 25 March, "I am sorry I did not make the matter plainer." It was made plain that *Dubliners* was, in a word, unpublishable.

The year 1914 was a good one. In January, Grant Richards must have assuaged his guilty conscience when he reconsidered *Dubliners* and agreed to its publication the following June. Also in 1914, Joyce began *Ulysses*.

Joyce transformed *Stephen Hero*, which he had written in 1904, into *A Portrait of the Artist as a Young Man*. After a gestation period of ten years, it emerged in serial form in *The Egoist*, a magazine edited by Harriet Shaw Weaver. The first installment appeared on 2 February 1914, his thirty-second birthday, and the final one on 15 September 1915, a period that should have facilitated book publication. But Grant Richards turned down *Portrait* in May 1915 on the grounds that an intelligent audience for it was not available in wartime. Martin Secker also was prompt in his refusal to publish it in volume form.

Duckworth was less prompt, taking several months before rebuffing *Portrait* in January 1916 and sending Joyce the reader's report in which Edward Garnett had evaluated it as being "tedious to the ordinary man among the reading public. . . .It is too discursive, formless, unrestrained, and ugly things, ugly words are too prominent." Eventually, after trying T. Werner Laurie and John Lane, after refusals by two American publishers including Yale University Press, and through the efforts of Harriet Weaver, B. W. Huebsch of New York accepted *A Portrait of the Artist as a Young Man*. The first edition was published in America in December 1916. It appeared in England the following year.

The search for a publisher for *Ulysses* was depressingly familiar. *The Little Review* accepted it in 1918 for serial publication, which ceased in the middle, when the editors were prosecuted for publishing obscene material. Ben Huebsch (who had published *Portrait* and *Dubliners* in 1916 and *Chamber Music* in 1918 as well as Joyce's only play, *Exiles,* after it too had undergone many rejections) decided not to take on *Ulysses*. Boni and Liveright joined the list of rejecters. *Ulysses* was offered to Leonard and Virginia Woolf who ran the Hogarth Press. Estimating two years to produce this lengthy book of three hundred pages, and concerned that both publisher and printer would be prosecuted for a book which Virginia described as "reeling with indecency," they declined the opportunity to have it emerge from their small handpress.

It was Sylvia Beach, who owned the Shakespeare and Company bookshop in Paris, who had the courage and vision to publish *Ulysses* in book form under the Shakespeare and Company imprint. It appeared as a banned book on his fortieth birthday, 2 February 1922 and, as a banned book, catapulted him to fame.

Pomes Penyeach (1927) and *Finnegans Wake* (1939) were his only books to be issued without the painful and protracted struggle for publication. By this time he was suffering from severe eye trouble and deteriorating health. The novelist who was born in Dublin in 1882 and spent most of his life abroad, died at fifty-eight, on 13 January 1941.

EDWARD LEAR

The publishers were unwilling to risk
one hundred pounds for the copyright to
Edward Lear's *Book of Nonsense.*

When Edward Lear published *A Book of Nonsense* in 1846,
neither he nor the publishers knew what the literary reper-
cussions would be.

Actually, his career as a nonsense writer began with
his career as an artist. After a difficult and deprived
childhood—he was born in 1812, the youngest of a family of
twenty-one children—he took up painting as a means of
earning his living. He found regular employment with the
Zoological Society in London making drawings of the parrots
at the Regent's Park Zoo and achieved a reputation for
accuracy and for beauty of design and execution as an
ornithological artist.

In 1832, the Earl of Derby, impressed with Lear's work at
the Zoo, invited him to the ancient and great family estate of
Knowsley Hall near Liverpool to make illustrations of his
unique collection of animals and birds for publication in a
book. Lear earned the lifelong patronage and friendship of the
noble family that gave its name to the famous horse race.

It was due to his work as an artist at Knowsley that he
inadvertently became a writer. He amused the children of the
house with his silly rhymes, and the nonsense he made up for

69

the Knowsley children eventually found the way into print. He perfected the limerick form and achieved fame as a popular and professional nonsense writer.

In 1846, the results of four years of work were printed in a private edition, *Gleanings from the Menagerie and Aviary at Knowsley Hall*; but that same year also saw publication of *A Book of Nonsense*, written by the "old Derry Down Derry, who loves to see little folks merry." Lear had made a belated decision, for unknown reasons, to publish the nonsense. Perhaps he submitted to pressure from friends who felt he should share the fun with other children. Or perhaps he hoped the profits would defray expenses for his sojourn abroad. In any case, the edition of seventy limericks in two volumes, printed by Thomas Maclean, with no mention of Lear's name, was to bring him the lasting fame and recognition that eluded him as an artist.

A second edition of *A Book of Nonsense* appeared ten years later. And in 1861 Lear decided to bring out a third edition, revised and enlarged, this time under his own name. This time too, based on the book's previous success, he could afford to feel more secure about finding a publisher instead of again producing it himself.

But his confidence was misplaced. Both Routledge and Smith Elder declined the book. He had offered to sell the copyright for one hundred pounds, but the publishers were unwilling to take any risk. Once again, Lear undertook its publication together with the entire cost of production. Now, with nothing to lose, Routledge offered to take a thousand copies for distribution.

When the edition sold out immediately, the publishers changed their minds about purchasing the copyright. So did Lear. Shrewdly, he thought, he raised the price. Neither he nor they appreciated its potential and value when he sold the copyright outright for a mere £125, the total profit he realized for a book that went into nearly thirty editions in his own lifetime. Perhaps this is one time when the publishers are not entirely to be blamed for failing to recognize the endearing and enduring appeal of Lear's nonsense verse, for neither did the author himself recognize the scroobious comic effects of his runcible poems.

Before he left England in August 1880, never to see his homeland again, he went on to produce other "volumes of stuff": *Nonsense Songs, Stories, Botany and Alphabets* (1871) and *More Nonsense* (1872). *Laughable Lyrics* appeared in 1877, the fourth and final nonsense book to be published in his lifetime. When he died on 29 January 1888, Edward Lear was famous, not as an artist, but as a best-selling author.

W. SOMERSET MAUGHAM

"There is some ability in this, but not *very*
much. . . . satire against society is not
deep enough or humorous enough. . .
fairy tale is not *striking* enough to
command attention."

A firm but courteous rejection from a publisher made a
novelist of Somerset Maugham. He began life on 25 January
1874 in Paris where his father was a solicitor to the British
embassy. His mother died when he was eight and his father
when he was ten. The insecure, stuttering lad was returned to
England to live with an uncle in Kent. He attended the King's
School in Canterbury, and he spent a significant year at
Heidelberg, where he wrote a biography of Meyerbeer.
Although he destroyed the manuscript after it was rejected by
a publisher, the experience gave him the unflinching desire to
take up writing as a profession.

Knowing with absolutely certainty that he wanted to be
a writer, Maugham elected to study medicine. It was a
profession to fall back on in case of failure as a writer, and
it was an opportunity to live in London. He trained at
St. Thomas's Hospital in Lambeth from 1892 to 1897 and
qualified as a doctor, but never practiced. He recorded
observations and conversations in a notebook he kept,
and he wrote two short stories—"Daisy" and "A Bad
Example"—which later appeared in a volume of his stories
called *Orientations* (1899), his third book.

While still a medical student, Maugham sent his two stories to T. Fisher Unwin in December 1898. The following June, the reader Edward Garnett declined "A Bad Example": "There is some ability in this, but not *very* much. Mr. Maugham has imagination, and he can write prettily but his satire against society is not deep enough or humorous enough, and his fairy tale is not *striking* enough to command attention. He should be advised to try the humbler magazines for a time, and if he tries anything more important to send it on to us."

On the basis of the reader's report, the publisher returned the stories saying they were not long enough for inclusion in his Pseudonym Library series, but he would consider any novel the writer might happen to have. Instead of viewing the rejection as a polite but final refusal, as anyone else might have done, Maugham viewed it as an opportunity to provide the publisher with the book he wanted and dashed off a letter to him announcing his intention. And he immediately began writing *Liza of Lambeth*, a novel based on the experiences and observations of the life he saw in London on his medical rounds. He later wrote in *The Summing Up*, "I do not know a better training for a writer than to spend some years in the medical profession."

Liza of Lambeth, the story of a young girl destroyed by the slum environment, was ready on 14 January 1897. This time a report by Vaughan Nash repudiated it: "The novel reveals the author's familiarity with the speech and customs of the London poor, but there is no indication that he knows how to use this knowledge effectively. Some details are revolting and unpublishable. . . and the incidents are unconvincing."

But this time Edward Garnett, the second reader, was receptive and praised its authenticity: "The temper and the tone of the book is wholesome and by no means morbid. The work is objective and both the atmosphere and the

73

environment of the mean district are unexaggerated. . ." He went on to warn that if Unwin did not publish it someone else would, and he shrewdly summed up Maugham as someone who "has insight and humour and will probably be heard of again."

A third reader, W. H. Chesson, seconded the enthusiastic endorsement and recommended publication of the "interesting, impressive and truthful" novel. Unwin accepted the advice and published *Liza* in September 1897, making Maugham an author at twenty-three.

For his next book, Maugham left slum fiction and wrote *The Making of a Saint* (1898). He also produced stories for periodicals—enough for the collection called *Orientations*, published by Fisher Unwin.

But Unwin refused *The Artistic Temperament of Stephen Carey*. Or rather, they refused the young author's lofty demand for an advance of £100. He took the manuscript to several other firms, but it was unwanted at any price. The novel remained unpublished, perhaps a fortunate circumstance, for he was to garner from it much of the material used in his later masterpiece, *Of Human Bondage*.

Despite failures and further rejections, Maugham did not collect on his insurance by returning to the medical profession to earn a living. He began instead, in 1898, to apply himself to his craft with great diligence, producing novels and plays as well as a travel book about Spain, *The Land of the Blessed Virgin*. It was rejected by Murray and Macmillan in 1901 but a new version was accepted by William Heinemann in February 1903.

Over the next nine years he produced six more novels. *The Hero* was published by Hutchinson in 1901. In 1902, after being refused by every major publisher including Hodder & Stoughton, *Mrs. Craddock* was taken on by William Heinemann, who published also his last volume exactly sixty years later. *The Merry-Go-Round* (1904) was his next minor novel. *Loaves and Fishes,* which had failed to find acceptance when it was first written as a play in 1902 (it waited until 1911 to be staged), he novelized as *The Bishop's Apron* in 1906. *The Explorer* (1907) was also based on a play. More bad luck came when Methuen accepted *The Magician* in 1906, giving him an advance, but then decided against publication, leaving the last of his half dozen unsuccessful novels to emerge from Heinemann's press in 1908.

Production continued also with minor plays and with minor setbacks. When his first London play, *A Man of Honour,* was presented on 22 February 1903, it lasted on the stage for two days. With his income at a low ebb, he considered returning to medicine, possibly as a ship's doctor, a position that would satisfy also his love of travel. But it never came to fruition. He simply wrote and rewrote.

The turning point came by chance in October 1907 when the manager of the Court Theatre needed a replacement for a failure he had on his hands and took on Maugham's *Lady Frederick.* The final scene dazzled the audience when the eponymous character deliberately disillusioned the besotted young man by revealing herself on stage without makeup and with unkempt hair, an unglamorous role turned down by a number of famous actresses. An enormous success, *Lady Frederick* made Maugham a famous playwright overnight.

Jack Straw followed shortly thereafter (March 1908) at the Vaudeville Theatre, while *Mrs. Dot* opened the following April at the Comedy Theatre and *The Explorer* at the Lyric Theatre the following June. With four plays running in London at the same time, he had achieved a resounding success as a popular and affluent playwright. He went on producing such theatre pieces as *East of Suez, The Circle, The Constant Wife, The Letter*—a total of some thirty plays.

He wrote also over twenty novels including *Of Human Bondage* (1915), *The Moon and Sixpence* (1919), *The Painted Veil* (1925), *Cakes and Ale* (1930), *The Razor's Edge* (1944), and *Then and Now* (1946). His last novel, *Catalina* (1962), he completed on his seventy-third birthday, fifty years after his first.

And forty-eight years after his first volume of short stories, *Orientations*, came his last volume of stories, *Creatures of Circumstance*—a total of one hundred stories in nine volumes. In Maugham's incredibly large output are travel books, autobiographical works, literary criticism, and essays on a variety of subjects.

Despite his detractors, despite critical objections or shortcomings in the vast body of written work left on his death in 1965, enough remains of great and enduring value to offer a lesson in tenacity in the face of early rejections. It was his good fortune—and ours—that kept him from relinquishing a writing career in favor of one in medicine.

As for his being the highest paid author for several decades, the great thing was the power that his financial independence gave him, as he later expressed it, to tell any publisher to go to hell.

GEORGE ORWELL

"What was needed . . . was not more
communism but more public-spirited
pigs."

Eric Arthur Blair, born in a remote town in India on 25 June
1903, became George Orwell when his first book, *Down and
Out in Paris and London*, was published in 1933. But first he
had to go through the painful obstacles blocking the road to
authorship.

When he was a year old, his mother returned to England
for the sake of the health and education of her children.
He attended school at St. Cyprian's, a hateful experience
recorded in *Such, Such Were the Joys*, and at fourteen went on
to Eton. He seemed to relinquish an early desire to be a writer
when he left England at nineteen to adopt a career as a police
officer in Burma.

After five years of colonial service, he returned home on
medical leave. In England, he announced almost immediately
his decision to resign from his career as a colonial officer in
Burma and devote himself to becoming an author. He moved
to London and struggled for five years to achieve publication.
He also decided, like so many aspiring young writers in the
1920s, to spend time in Paris.

He remained in Paris for some twenty months,
experiencing poverty and even enduring three days of

starvation when his money was stolen. He became ill with pneumonia and spent some weeks in a hospital. But from Parisian streets he gleaned material that makes up the first part of *Down and Out in Paris and London*.

In Paris he managed also to write two novels and short stories, but his fiction remained unwanted by any publisher. By the time he left in December 1929, only half a dozen small journalistic pieces had appeared in print. In *Down and Out in Paris and London*, which focuses on his last months in the French capital, he describes a Russian friend he met there who gave this practical advice: "Writing is bosh. There is only one way to make money at writing, and that is to marry a publisher's daughter." Recalling in later years the unprinted short stories and novels he wrote during his time in Paris, he expressed regret that he had destroyed so much of his work.

Shortly after returning to England, in December 1929, the *Adelphi* accepted an article and began a long association with Orwell. He became a regular contributor and developed a lifelong friendship with Sir Richard Rees, who ran the monthly magazine.

He worked on *Down and Out* and, for the sake of his book, immersed himself in the squalor of the poorest segment of society. He made forays into London's East End disguised as a tramp and shared the life of destitutes in order to learn at first hand all about conditions in the world of abject poverty. His experiences became the raw material for the book. In the autumn of 1930 he submitted the manuscript to Jonathan Cape. It was rejected for being "too short and fragmentary." He made revisions, expanding it and abolishing the diary technique, and resubmitted the new version. It was again rejected.

Sir Richard Rees, believing the manuscript had merit, advised him to keep on trying and offered to recommend it to a friend and editor at Faber & Faber—T. S. Eliot. The aspiring author approached Eliot timidly, at first proposing a translation of a French novel about a prostitute rather than his own book. Nothing ever came of it. Not until December did Orwell find the courage to submit his own book to Eliot.

Then he waited. And waited. While he waited, Leonard Moore, a literary agent, contacted him and offered to represent him. Orwell informed him that his work was being considered by Faber and "if they won't have it I doubt whether anyone else would, as it was sent to T. S. Eliot with a personal recommendation from a friend of his."

He waited impatiently through January and half of February before telephoning to ask whether a decision had been made. The typescript had not yet even been read, he was told, but Eliot "would have a look at it shortly." Again he waited, until the suspense ended with the arrival of a letter two days later: "We did find it of very great interest, but I regret to say that it does not appear to me possible as a publishing venture." The great poet had signed his name to a letter filled with the clichéd phrases of rejection.

Professional rejection led to personal rejection with concomitant abandonment of the manuscript that he gave to his friend and guiding spirit, Mabel Fierz, asking her to discard it. The matter of authorship might have ended there if she were not the kind of friend that every disappointed writer needs. She saw its value and undertook, not to burn it as instructed, but to get it published on his behalf.

Mrs. Fierz took it to Leonard Moore, insisting that the literary agent read it and consider taking it on. Moore did like it and did offer to find a publisher. Grateful, but lacking self-confidence, the author made the condition that if it were ever to find a taker, the book must be issued under a pseudonym "as I am not proud of it." A few months later he settled on a solid old English first name and a surname that recalls the river that meandered near his Southwold family home in Suffolk—George Orwell.

Another period of waiting was this time followed by good news. Victor Gollancz, a relatively new publisher in business for only four years, would accept if the author would agree to tone down the language and make certain changes to avoid libel. Orwell agreed. A contract arrived in August 1932 with the eleemosynary advance of £40, not enough to permit him to give up his teaching position. But the first-time author had no objections. Published on 9 January 1933, the book received generally very favorable reviews, and the pseudonym, now an asset, stuck. Orwell reacted by making good progress on *Burmese Days*, a novel he had in mind since his days in the Indian Imperial Police. The natural course was for Gollancz to take on his second book.

But Victor Gollancz, having recently experienced a libel suit for another book, felt vulnerable and fearful of any possible lawsuits that might be brought by the author's old friends in Burma on appearance of this book; the firm's solicitor vetoed *Burmese Days*. Heinemann, for the same reason, also rejected it. Gollancz eventually did publish it, but only after an American publisher, Harper's, took the risk first.

Harper's tactfully requested changes to mitigate the possibility of libel accusations. Government employees became businessmen, for example, to avoid any suggestion of an attack on British imperialism. Legal advisers approved, and Orwell's first novel was first issued in America on 25 October 1934. Happily, it never became enmeshed in libel action.

A Clergyman's Daughter was the next novel. Gollancz again considered this second novel, again anxious about potential libel. Orwell agreed to make necessary changes, and Gollancz accepted, asking also to see *Burmese Days* again. When Orwell acquiesced to certain changes, Gollancz agreed to bring out the revised version in June.

Now Gollancz harried him for *Keep the Aspidistra Flying*. Published in April 1936, the novel did not do well, and an American edition did not appear until 1956, six years after the author's death. But after he submitted the manuscript, the publisher asked him to write about living conditions in the North of England, and the result was *The Road to Wigan Pier*, issued in 1936.

Gollancz did not want *Homage to Catalonia*, but Frederic Warburg of Secker and Warburg requested the documentary account of Orwell's war experience in Spain and published what turned out to be a commercial failure.

A contract gave Gollancz the option on the next three novels. Orwell had to submit *Coming up for Air* but, having previously given in to demands and criticisms, now refused to make changes. To his surprise, the novel was accepted outright and published less than two months later, on 12 June 1939, the last Orwell novel with the Gollancz imprint.

Gollancz, who had the right of first refusal, refused the next novel, the bestseller that gave George Orwell worldwide acclaim and established his name indelibly as a major writer—*Animal Farm*. Politics had interfered with the decision. Gollancz could not tolerate the anti-Soviet position and did not want to offend the Soviet dictator. He commented years later: "We couldn't have published it then. Those people were fighting for us and had just saved our necks at Stalingrad."

Three other publishers were just as quick to turn it down. Also for political reasons, Nicholson and Watson refused it. Then, with Gollancz insisting that his option was valid for the next two novels because *Animal Farm* was not a full-length work, Jonathan Cape decided not to take on an author who had commitments elsewhere,

The third publisher was Faber and Faber. T. S. Eliot, given an opportunity to repeat the rejection route he had taken thirteen years earlier, outdid himself. His cold letter declining *Animal Farm* missed the point: "Your pigs are far more intelligent than the other animals, and therefore the best qualified to run the farm... What was needed (someone might argue) was not more communism but more public-spirited pigs." Eliot, at Faber and Faber since 1925, had become known as "the Pope of Russell Square." But he made mistakes.

Convinced that it was not likely to be accepted, Orwell considered having the book privately printed before giving it to Fredric Warburg, who accepted almost immediately. Although Warburg made a definite commitment and paid an advance of £100, the small firm had a problem with paper supplies and rationing, and publication was delayed until after Hitler was defeated and the need to defend Stalin was diminished—until 17 August 1945.

The results were astounding. A first printing of a mere 4,500 copies (the paper shortage must have been acute) soon sold out. In November came a second printing of 10,000 copies, and the book sold over 25,000 hardcover copies in the first five years.

American publication came a year later, after rejection by more than a dozen firms including Harper, Knopf, Viking, and Scribner, presumably on political grounds. However, Dial Press felt there was no market for animal stories. Harcourt Brace brought it out in August 1946, and it was a Book-of-the-Month Club selection. Sales reached 590,000 in four years. Reviews were sensational, and the author was compared with Voltaire and Swift. He was established as a major English writer, and *Animal Farm* became an international bestseller.

Even greater success came when *Nineteen Eighty-Four* appeared three years later, brought out on both sides of the Atlantic in June 1949. Victor Gollancz released him from his contract on Orwell's insistence, and it went to Secker and Warburg. The American rights went to Harcourt Brace, and it was again a Book-of-the-Month Club selection.

While writing the book, Orwell was seriously ill with tuberculosis. After a lifetime of struggling to overcome poverty and rejection and make a living as a writer, he had little time to enjoy the enormous adulation and remuneration finally accorded him. He died on 21 January 1950. He was forty-six.

BEATRIX POTTER

"As it is too late to produce a book for
this season, we think it best to decline
your kind offer at any rate for this year."

Although she was born in a genteel district of London on
28 July 1866, Beatrix Potter is associated with the English
Lake District, specifically with Hill Top (now a National Trust
property) in the village of Sawrey. It was from this favorite
place that she was encouraged to write and publish her first
little book for children.

The story of that book is reminiscent of Lewis Carroll's
Alice in Wonderland, which also began as a tale for a special
child. Beatrix Potter had remained attached to her former
governess even after Miss Annie Carter became Mrs. Moore
and the mother of a large family. When five-year-old Noël
Moore fell ill and was confined to bed for months, Beatrix
Potter wrote a letter to him, dated 4 September 1893, which
contained a story of her rabbit Peter, enhanced by her own
little pictures: "Dear Noël, I don't know what to write to you,
so I shall tell you a story about four little rabbits, whose names
are Flopsy, Mopsy, Cottontail and Peter. . . ."

Fortunately, Noël had kept that letter and was able to
relinquish it when she decided, eight years later, to copy it,
revise and enlarge it, and send it to the publishers, Frederick

Warne & Company—who promptly rejected it. In fact, in the year 1900 it was rejected by at least six publishers.

Beatrix Potter felt exasperation rather than despair and, with no prospective publisher in sight, decided to print the book privately. Resolute, she used her savings to bring out an edition of two hundred fifty copies of *Peter Rabbit* in December 1901. Some she gave away as gifts, others she sold at a nominal price, six pence in today's money, to great aunts and great friends. One happy owner of the book was Conan Doyle, whose children derived great pleasure from it. The edition sold out, and a second printing of two hundred copies soon followed.

Meanwhile, Canon Hardwicke Rawnsley, himself a writer and a family friend who had offered to find a publisher for her, again contacted Frederick Warne in September 1901. To the specialists in children's books, he again offered the Peter Rabbit story. But this time he had written an alternative version of the story in his own verse. The publisher again politely declined stating a preference for the "simple narration" and insisting on the necessity of colored pictures.

Beatrix had previously offered black-and-white sketches, reasoning that color printing would be prohibitively expensive as well as dull, since shades were mostly browns and greens. Warne concluded, "as it is too late to produce a book for this season, we think it best to decline your kind offer at any rate for this year."

Warne's courteous refusal did, however, indicate at least a modicum of interest. On their insistence that a book with colored pictures could in fact be produced at a price affordable to children—she wanted the purchase price to be no more than a shilling—Beatrix relented and resubmitted the story the following year with colored illustrations. Warne reconsidered, and her writing career was launched.

Before the publication date of 2 October 1902, the entire first edition of eight thousand copies had been sold. Her simple prose, exquisite pictures, and good stories, based on her own knowledge of animals, added up to a formula for huge success. By the end of 1903 *Peter Rabbit* had sold 50,000 copies.

Other tales followed. Of the thirteen books she produced, six are concerned with the setting, activities, and people of Hill Top and Sawrey, in which she delighted. Her children's fantasy world became extremely popular, and the financial success enabled her to buy Hill Top Farm. Such was the success and influence of her writing that even her marriage can be indirectly attributed to her success with *Peter Rabbit*.

With the proceeds of her books, she purchased in 1909 Castle Farm, which could be seen from Hill Top and which had a field adjoining Hill Top property. The transaction was handled by the solicitor William Heelis, and she became Mrs. William Heelis in October 1913. Mrs. Heelis of Sawrey was a wife, farmer, and happy resident of the Lake District for the next thirty years—until her death on 22 December 1943 at the age of seventy-seven. And, thanks to her publishing perseverance, Hill Top has become a place of pilgrimage for the vast numbers of children who continue to delight in her books.

BARBARA PYM

"In present conditions we could not sell
a sufficient number of copies to cover
costs, let alone to make any profit."

One of the most remarkable stories in modern publishing—
with fairy-tale elements of rediscovery, victory over despair,
and rise to fame and fortune—centers on a *Times Literary
Supplement* poll of 1977 in which both Lord David Cecil and
Philip Larkin selected Barbara Pym as one of the most
underrated novelists of the century. The survey created a
resurgence of interest.

Barbara Pym had attained respect as an author whose six
successful novels had appeared between 1950 and 1961. She
was on the verge of even wider recognition when her work
suddenly and inexplicably became anathema to publishers.
Everything she wrote after 1961 was rejected, and a
sixteen-year period of silence ensued. Now, thanks to the two
perceptive appraisals, her status as an important novelist was
restored. She became a center of media attention, and the
public demanded more novels. She happily acquiesced,
completing three new books before her death in 1980: *Quartet
in Autumn*, *The Sweet Dove Died*, and *A Few Green Leaves*
(published posthumously).

Even the start of Barbara Pym's career represented an
uneasy rise to success. Born on 2 June 1913 in Oswestry,

Shropshire, Barbara Pym knew by the time she went to Oxford in 1931 that she would be a writer. Indeed, the tall, attractive Shropshire lass began a novel in 1934 using herself, her sister, and people in her Oxford circle as prototypes for her fictional characters and referred to it as "my novel of real people." But for her first novel, the girl of twenty-two displayed unusual daring in projecting the main characters into their fifties. In later novels, she was to make the uneventful lives of spinsters and ordinary people eventful and full of surprises. Philip Larkin commended her "unique eye and ear for the small poignancies and comedies of everyday life."

She finished her first novel, *Some Tame Gazelle*, in November 1935 and sent it to Chatto and Windus and to Gollancz. Both publishers rejected it. She sent it to Cape, and an encouraging letter from Jonathan Cape in August 1936 offered the hope of publication if she would make certain minor changes. She complied, made the alterations, and returned the manuscript, expressing in her diary a certain amount of protective cynicism. After all, Macmillan and Methuen had also refused it. Her hopes were completely dashed when Jonathan Cape replied with regret that, although he liked it, successful publication was in doubt due to the lack of "unanimity of appreciation for the book's chances."

Devastated, she put the novel aside until after the war, when she revised it again and again sent it to Jonathan Cape. This time *Some Tame Gazelle* was accepted and published in 1950. So the author who had begun writing novels at sixteen, was finally published at thirty-seven.

Five more novels followed: *Excellent Women, Jane and Prudence, Less than Angels, A Glass of Blessings*, and *No Fond Return of Love*. The six novels, all published by Cape between

1950 and 1961, enjoyed modest financial success and good critical reviews.

She was working on a new novel, *An Unsuitable Attachment*, when the poet Philip Larkin wrote to her praising her work and offering to write a review article about her next novel. "It will be my seventh," Barbara Pym responded, "which seems a significant number." She might more accurately have used the adjective "inauspicious" to describe her seventh novel. She had worried about the title and kept several alternatives in store. But she need not have been anxious. Cape rejected the novel outright, and Philip Larkin had a long wait for her next novel.

Unlucky in love—she never married—she was also unlucky in a career filled with cruel and undeserved disappointment. Cape turned down the ill-fated novel, citing increased costs and difficulties in publishing fiction, not even suggesting revisions as they had done in the past. The letter of rejection stated that they "unanimously reached the sad conclusion that in present conditions we could not sell a sufficient number of copies to cover costs, let alone to make any profit." Wren Howard continued, "You will, I am sure, appreciate how distasteful it is for me to have to write to you in this strain after publishing your novels and always having maintained a particularly friendly author/publisher relationship, but in fairness to one's company and to my colleagues I feel I cannot do otherwise."

Perhaps because Jonathan Cape himself had died, perhaps because the novel was not as good as her previous ones, the callous and greedy new staff at Cape, with complete insensitivity, dismissed all she had written as well as anything she might write in the future.

Crushed by the bitter blow of a blank rejection by the publisher of her previous six successful novels, her self-confidence completely shattered, she was left to cope with feelings of failure and inadequacy and to face the fact that she was not an established writer, after all.

The novel was offered to others, but Macmillan found *An Unsuitable Attachment* unsuitable for their list. Longmans and Faber also refused it, as did all the firms who saw it. And Barbara Pym remained unpublishable with little likelihood that her novels would ever again be printed. When, some twenty years later, the novel was issued posthumously in Britain and in America, the Washington *Post* wrote with hindsight: "The publisher must have been mad to reject this jewel." Robert Liddell likened it to Jane Austen's *Northanger Abbey*, another rejected novel with a flawed structure, a posthumous book which has enriched the world, while A. L. Rowse dubbed her "a contemporary Jane Austen."

Nevertheless, during the sixteen-year hiatus, she kept notebooks in which she recorded observations and ideas. She remained committed to her art and faced the demoralizing situation by continuing to write. In 1968 she completed *The Sweet Dove Died* and sent it off under various titles to several publishers (Chatto, Macmillan, Mcdonald, Peter Davies, Constable, Cassell), even selecting a pseudonym several times in the vain hope that "Tom Crampton" would be a more appealing, more creditable, name. But it made no difference; her new novels were simply repudiated. "Not the kind of novel to which people are turning," wrote one publisher.

The public, however, continued to remember and admire her works, and she retained popularity with a loyal and enthusiastic readership. Her books remained on library shelves. The BBC serialized *No Fond Return of Love* in 1965, and a critical appreciation of her work in *Ariel* magazine in 1971 referred to "her wit and her sense of the ridiculous which make her books both delicious and distinguished." She persevered in the hope of being accepted again one day and completed another novel about four elderly and obscure office workers in the throes of retirement. Later entitled *Quartet in Autumn,* this novel too was rejected by Hamish Hamilton and several others.

In April 1975 she finally met Philip Larkin, with whom she had been corresponding since the generous offer he had made some fourteen years earlier to review her book. Like the fateful meeting of C. S. Lewis with Joy Davidman (as depicted in the play and film called *Shadowlands*) this meeting also took place at the Randolph Hotel in Oxford, a venue which must surely be singled out for events of great literary significance. Barbara Pym recorded the pleasurable lunch they had "sitting in the window looking out towards the Ashmolean. . ." Larkin became a good friend and remained a source of comfort and encouragement to the end of her life.

Not long afterwards came the vindication and triumphant reappearance of Barbara Pym, novelist. She was cast into the literary limelight by the *Times Literary Supplement* symposium of 21 January 1977 rating her as one of the great novelists of the century. The enthusiastic praise was reiterated the following day on the front page of the London *Times.* The resurrection of her name and reputation resulted in publication of new novels and reissue of old ones.

Macmillan offered to publish *Quartet in Autumn.* Cape, not realizing they had already recently rejected it, now rushed in to inquire about *Quartet* and had to settle for reprinting her earlier novels. Thankfully, she at last achieved success and acclaim. But no thanks are due the publishers, the greedy beneficiaries who should have been the generous benefactors.

The year 1977 was her *annus mirabilis.* Barbara Pym, celebrity, was widely interviewed. She was broadcast on Radio Oxford and several other programs including the BBC's "Desert Island Discs." The BBC made a television film about her life and work. That year Philip Larkin published another article on her work in the *Times Literary Supplement.* Articles appeared in the *Times* and *Guardian,* and tributes poured in.

Macmillan brought out *Quartet in Autumn* in September of that year to enormous praise. The book won worldwide acclaim and was shortlisted in October for the prestigious Booker Prize. *The Sweet Dove Died* appeared the following year.

Barbara Pym was amused and delighted to learn that in America, where she was published by Dutton, she was "being taught in an American university!" The attention she was now receiving made her express a concern for "other good writers in the wilderness who deserve the sort of treatment I'm now getting."

Finally, she was established as a major novelist. But recognition came late to Barbara Pym. She had only three years in which to enjoy her newfound fame before she died of cancer early in 1980.

AYN RAND

"In its present form . . . the book is
unsalable and unpublishable."

Like many established writers, Ayn Rand decided to be a
writer when she was a child—in fact, in 1914 at the age of nine.
An oeuvre that includes *The Fountainhead* and *Atlas Shrugged*
provides clear evidence that she achieved overwhelming
success in her mission.

Born Alice Rosenbaum in St. Petersburg on 2 February
1905, she left Russia at twenty-one to live with relatives in
Chicago, bringing with her to the new country her unyielding
determination to become an author. She did not remain long
in Chicago. The events that led to her emergence on the first
rung of the writing ladder are as unreal as a scenario of a
Hollywood Grade B movie that she herself might have
composed.

Not yet proficient in the language of her adopted country,
she decided to write scenarios for silent films and left for
Hollywood. She had the good fortune of meeting Cecil B.
De Mille, who offered her a job as an extra in a movie he was
shooting and invited her to learn about film making. And on
the set, she had the good fortune of meeting the actor Frank
O'Connor who became her devoted husband in a marriage
that lasted fifty years, until his death in 1979 at the age of
eighty-two.

In Hollywood, she became a junior screenwriter and worked to support herself at a variety of odd jobs from waitress to wardrobe mistress. She also produced four scenarios, all of which were unfortunately and immediately rejected. A fifth scenario was considered before that too was declined. She turned from writing outlines to script writing.

Having begun in 1930 her first novel, *We the Living*, she interrupted it the following year to write a full-length, original screenplay for money that she hoped would enable her to spend time on the novel. Universal Pictures bought the script of *Red Pawn* in 1932, but the film was never produced. She worked also on her own first play, *The Night of January 16th* and completed it in 1933 before returning to the novel, also completed by the end of that year.

We the Living, an extraordinary first novel, was begun only four years after her arrival in America when she painstakingly wrote, like Joseph Conrad, in a new language. The book was her response to a young man's admonition as she prepared to leave the country of her birth: "Tell them that Russia is a vast prison, and that we are all dying slowly."

One publishing house after another returned the novel, sometimes because it was too concerned with ideas and intellect, sometimes—it denounced Soviet Russia—for political reasons. With *We the Living* unsold and with her money running out, she was lucky enough to receive an offer for *The Night of January 16th*, a courtroom drama that enjoyed a successful Broadway run of seven months. It was during tryouts of the play in Philadelphia that a telegram arrived advising that the Macmillan Company had accepted *We the Living*.

The novel was published in March 1936. She sent a copy to Cecil B. De Mille with the inscription: "From a little Russian immigrant to whom he gave her first chance at writing."

Critical reviews were disappointing, and sales were slow at first. She complained that Macmillan did not publicize it and did "NOTHING" for it. It was lapsing into oblivion. Then, a year after publication, sales suddenly began to climb in a reversal of the usual expectation of high sales at first, then diminution. People were reading it, talking about it, and recommending it, until the edition of three thousand copies sold out. But Macmillan, considering the book a lost cause, had destroyed the type, thereby obviating the possibility of a reprint. She had earned a mere one hundred dollars from royalties.

Not until 1959 was *We the Living* reissued by Random House. The following year, a New American Library paperback edition sold over 400,000 copies in a single year—twenty-four years after the original date of publication and after the success of her two best known works, *The Fountainhead* and *Atlas Shrugged*.

In New York, while awaiting production of her play, she completed *Anthem*, a novelette she had in mind while still in Russia. Consistently rejected by American publishers, it first appeared in England in 1938, published by Cassell. But it continued to be unwanted in America, where it did not appear until 1946, after the phenomenal success of *The Fountainhead*.

But even *The Fountainhead* had difficulty finding its way into print. Submitted in 1940, it was rejected during the next two years by no less than a dozen publishing houses. Macmillan made an offer, but the author insisted on expenditure of money for publicity and advertising lest, like *We the Living*, it reach an early demise. They refused and ended the association.

Knopf offered a contract with an advance of a thousand dollars payable on completion of the manuscript. She worked hard, long hours but was not ready when the deadline of a year was due. Knopf agreed to an extension but would not pay the advance, and the contract was abandoned by mutual consent. The manuscript went back into circulation, back to another round of rejections.

Her agent, unable to sell *The Fountainhead*, attributed its major shortcoming to an unsympathetic hero. The author responded that Faulkner too had used unsympathetic central characters. But the strain of failure to sell the manuscript broke the relationship and left her without an agent or a publisher.

Publishers simply feared commercial failure. They refused it on grounds of too much intellectualism or too much political controversy or too much improbability. What it did not have too much of, they feared, was commercial possibility.

A story editor of Paramount Pictures, where Ayn Rand was working as a reader, offered to recommend it to any publisher of her choice. She chose Little, Brown for its good reputation with serious novels. They praised the novel but refused it, despite the influential patronage. The editor's message plunged her into the lowest point of dejection: "I wish there were an audience for a book of this kind. But there isn't. It won't sell." To have it rejected, she said, "because of its *greatness*—because it's *too good*—that's really a feeling of horror."

Her advocate at Paramount offered to submit it to another house of her choice, and she selected this time Bobbs-Merrill, where the young editor, Archibald G. Ogden, was enormously impressed. However, because she had requested an advance payment of twelve hundred dollars on royalties plus a year's time for completion, he had to send the manuscript to the head office in Indianapolis for authorization. The head of Bobbs-Merrill vetoed it when two readers turned it down firmly and decisively. Ogden, risking his position, wired an equally firm ultimatum: "If this is not the book for you, then I am not the editor for you." The director relented.

An interesting digression obviates any possible belief that Ogden had an infallible knack of picking winners, for this very same editor rejected Dale Carnegie's *How to Win Friends and Influence People.*

Ayn Rand was lucky when, in December 1941, a contract was signed. Just one week later, Pearl Harbor was bombed, and the contract might not have gone through in wartime. *The Fountainhead* was completed on 31 December 1942, just making its deadline, and published in May 1943 to excellent critical reviews. Not an instant best-seller, sales grew to enormous proportions as individuals read it and recommended it. With fifty thousand dollars for the film rights, she achieved financial security, and she returned to Hollywood to write the screen adaptation.

Ayn Rand went on to write *Atlas Shrugged.* Incredibly, Bobbs-Merrill, who had rights to it on the basis of a contract for *The Fountainhead*, was not satisfied with the book. Ross Baker discussed their complaints: "The book is *much* too long. The editors and I have made a long list of possible cuts." Ayn refused to make changes, and the publisher withdrew: "In its present form, I regret to say that the book is unsalable and unpublishable."

With Bobbs-Merrill out of the picture, almost every other major publisher approached her to express interest. She narrowed the possibilities to four: McGraw-Hill, Knopf, Viking, and Random House. When she finally selected Random House, Bennett Cerf responded with "It's a great book. Name your own terms." The publication date was 10 October 1957.

It had taken her eleven years to complete the novel that began with the question, "Who is John Galt?" In the spring of 1957, when Random House was bringing out *Atlas Shrugged*, she gave the advice which undoubtedly accounts for her success: "Don't ever give up what you want in life. The struggle is worth it."

Atlas Shrugged sold over a million copies a few years after its publication in 1957 and continues to sell in vast numbers. Her novels have been translated into over a dozen foreign languages and continue to be read and studied at universities. They sell over three hundred thousand copies a year, more than most new bestsellers, and have sold over twenty million copies.

But *Atlas Shrugged* was her last novel, marking the end of her career as a writer of fiction. Afterwards, she turned to the world of ideas, writing only works on philosophy and giving lectures, until her death in 1982. The books that were rejected for having no commercial possibilities have become modern classics.

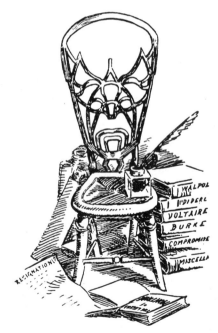

DOROTHY L. SAYERS

Her first novel was turned down because
of "coarseness."

A writer of detective novels, poetry, religious dramas and
articles, translator of Dante, and popular lecturer, Dorothy
Leigh Sayers was born in Oxford on 13 June 1893. But she
grew up in various places in the fens of East Anglia, and, at
fifteen, was sent to the Godolphin School in Salisbury. It was
a complete circle back to Oxford when she received a
scholarship for Somerville College, later to become the model
for Shrewsbury College in *Gaudy Night*. She completed her
studies in modern languages as an honors graduate. But a
degree was not granted until 1920, when it became
permissible to award degrees to women.

At Oxford, Dorothy was a brilliant scholar, if somewhat
boisterous and rebellious. Her dons recognized her academic
ability but recorded that she should have shown more interest
in subjects like mathematics which she found unappealing.
She was considered "lacking somewhat in self-restraint." A
Miss Bruce stated that "she has a good critical power, but
strikes me as being somewhat wanting in imagination." In
view of the writer who emerged and the books she created,
that comment shows about as much insight as was shown by
the publishers who rejected *Whose Body*?

After graduation, with no interest in a teaching career, she had great difficulty finding suitable regular work for herself. She held a teaching position at Hull High School for girls for a year but found it unsatisfying. More satisfying was her position as a reader for Basil Blackwell, the Oxford publisher and bookseller. When Eric Whelpton asked her to join him at the Ecole des Roches in Normandy as a bilingual secretary and assistant, she accepted. After a year in France, she returned to England in 1920 to try to earn a living in London.

Plagued by financial anxieties, she searched for employment and took on another brief stint of teaching. She reasoned that writing detective fiction could be the best means for earning the most money and created her famous detective-hero, Lord Peter Wimsey. He materialized with apparent ease, she explained, for he simply "walked in, complete with spats, and applied in an airy don't-care-if-I-get-it way for the job of hero."

The second son of the late Duke of Denver shared her own tastes for scholarship, languages, good music, and fine wine. Blessed with wit, elegant manners, and talent, he could play piano and harpsichord, punt a boat, swim, dance, or play cricket. A slightly arrogant figure who sported a monocle, Lord Peter was also a lovable and intriguing personality who did eventually bring fame and fortune to his creator.

But first the manuscript had to be typed and readied for submission to a publisher. Struggling with poverty, she relied on her father for a loan. He paid the bill for what she called a "shaky investment." Her insecurity is expressed in her own words, "I've written a silly book, but I don't suppose any publisher will take it." She was very nearly right, for the very first words uttered by Lord Peter in the opening of *Whose Body?* contributed to the novel's rejection: " 'Oh, damn!' said Lord Peter Wimsey."

Actually, her first novel was turned down by several publishers because of "coarseness" which went beyond even the unacceptable opening. The story hinges on the disappearance of Sir Reuben Levy, a Jewish financier. When a naked corpse turns up in a bath, Inspector Sugg is eager to identify him as Levy. Originally, the hero dismissed the identification as a "no go by the evidence of my own eyes." And what was the evidence of his own eyes? The body was uncircumcised. Thus, Levy might not be dead—but the book was.

To overcome the indelicacy and clean up the book for publication, the author changed her device. She insured that the body could not be mistaken for that of the rich gentleman by giving it callused hands, blistered feet, decayed teeth, dirty ears, and filthy toenails—throwing in fleabites for definitive confirmation—and returned to the disheartening ordeal of getting the book accepted.

By November 1921, she was able to report that a publisher was showing interest in Lord Peter and felt confident enough to send the manuscript off to another publisher lest, in her desperate financial straits, she be tempted to accept unsatisfactory terms. She made a deal, not with a publisher, but with her parents. If they would only support her until the following summer, if Lord Peter was still floundering in search of a publisher, she would give up the idea of writing. She would consider herself beaten and take a permanent position as a teacher.

Meanwhile, the hassle for publication of *Whose Body?* continued. By April 1922 she found an agent to handle it for her. Good fortune came in May when she was hired as a copywriter at Benson's advertising agency. There she was happily employed for nine years in the production of such projects as the great mustard campaign,

Summer approached. Finally, in July, came an offer from the American publishing firm of Boni & Liveright. They were willing to take the risk of producing the book on condition that certain aspects were eliminated. The British firm of Dickinson had been dickering but withdrew in light of the prestigious offer from America, an offer that pleased her mightily.

Whose Body? was published in New York in 1923. T. Fisher Unwin bought the British publication rights and brought out the book by the end of the year. Sales were encouraging and led to a second Wimsey novel, *Clouds of Witness* (1926). And a third, *Unnatural Death* (1927). And so on—through *Five Red Herrings* (1931) and *The Nine Tailors* (1934) and ending with *Busman's Honeymoon* (1937), the last Wimsey novel. Lord Peter was engaged for fifteen years, tripping his way through twelve novels, three volumes of short stories, a play, and numerous articles—and bringing prosperity and fame to his creator.

The twelve novels of Dorothy L. Sayers have found a permanent place in literature, and the author is certainly among the top half dozen writers in the genre. How could those early publishers possibly have imagined a literary world without Peter Wimsey! As final testimony to her respectable standing, consider the last words spoken by Lord Peter in the last novel: "Oh damn!"

GEORGE BERNARD SHAW

*". . .it suffers, in our opinion, from the
fatal effect on a novel, of not being
interesting."*

That the writings of perhaps the greatest writer of the century
were refused and derogatory words spoken against his
creative endeavors, gives one pause.

When he was twenty, George Bernard Shaw left Dublin,
where he was born in 1856, to join his mother in London and
become a writer. He studied and read in the British Museum
Reading Room and became particularly attracted to socialism.
He worked at a variety of jobs and eventually became a
successful journalist, writing book reviews and art, music,
and theatre criticism. But he underwent a long literary
apprenticeship, and not until he was thirty-five did he arrive.

Before earning income as a critic, before becoming an
excellent public speaker and producing political and
economic pamphlets for the Fabian Society, he sought
employment and turned to writing, producing five novels
between 1879 and 1883.

Eleven publishers rejected his first novel, *Immaturity*,
named "with merciless fitness" he later said. Shaw first sent it
off on 8 November 1879 to Hurst Blackett, who returned it so
promptly that just five days later Kegan Paul was given the
opportunity to turn it down. Sampson Low would not even

deign to read it, Chapman and Hall refused it, and Macmillan considered it "unattractive." Another publisher offered to produce it on payment of a hundred pounds. While *Immaturity* was undergoing a round of regular rejections, Shaw continued to seek work and took a position with the Edison Telephone Company.

The central flaw of the novel is that a large number of conventional characters go on and on rather pointlessly. Perhaps Shaw's only point was that having found nothing else to do, he decided to become a writer and obstinately persisted in the task. He submitted a few articles to the new editor of the *Pall Mall Gazette*, and John Morley advised him to leave journalism. He left the Edison Company instead and started a new novel.

In December 1880, he finished *The Irrational Knot*, a shorter book with a more believable hero and defined plot, and sent the more promising novel off in search of a publisher. The Macmillan reader reported that it was "a novel of the most disagreeable kind... the whole idea of it is odd, perverse and crude. It is the work of a man writing about life when he knows nothing of it." The reader advised that publication "is out of the question. There is far too much adultery and like matters." On the grounds of morality, an American publisher also rejected it. Other repudiations of *The Irrational Knot* came from Richard Bentley and Sons, Smith Elder, Blackwood's, and William Heinemann, who kindly advised him not to send it to anyone else.

Meanwhile, Shaw continued to write articles and stories for magazines and received a steady stream of rejections. To attain publication, he even reversed a common female practice of using male names (as did the Brontë sisters) and tried a female pseudonym. But no acceptances came, and no income.

He wrote two more novels, *Love Among the Artists* and *Cashel Byron's Profession.* Although Edward Garnett of Fisher Unwin believed that *Love Among the Artists* deserved to be published, he advised against it because "few people would understand it, & few papers would praise it." Bentley's rejection of the book informed Shaw that it lacked interest for the "general reader." Shaw informed Bentley that he underestimated the "general reader." Yet he sent *Cashel Byron* to Bentley, where it was carefully perused by three readers before being rejected.

In America, Harper refused *Cashel Byron*, then—with no copyright law in existence to protect the author—published a pirated edition in 1886, offering Shaw ten pounds in compensation.

He started his fifth novel, *An Unsocial Socialist,* when he was twenty-seven and in December 1883 submitted the first English Marxian novel to Kegan Paul, Trench & Company, who replied: "It appears to us written in good style and language, but it suffers, in our opinion, from the fatal effect on a novel, of not being interesting." A second publisher, Smith Elder & Company, seconded that opinion: "We are afraid that the subscribers to the circulating libraries are not much interested in Socialism." It was refused also by David Douglas of Edinburgh and Chatto & Windus of London. John Morley of Macmillan, apparently forgetting that he had advised Shaw to abandon writing, now recognized the author's power as a writer—"pointed, rapid, forcible, sometimes witty, often powerful and occasionally eloquent"—but declined the novel because "the socialistic irony would not be attractive to many readers."

Instead of collecting more rejections from more publishers, an exasperated Shaw sent the manuscript to *To-Day* magazine for serialization. *An Unsocial Socialist* appeared between March and December 1884, without payment to the author. At least his name was before the public.

Serialization of *Cashel Byron's Profession* followed between April 1885 and March 1886. The printer, H. H. Champion, was so enthusiastic that he put out a Modern Press edition of two thousand five hundred copies in March 1886, and *Cashel Byron's Profession* became Shaw's first published book.

His two other novels, *The Irrational Knot* and *Love Among the Artists*, were also published serially. *An Unsocial Socialist* was produced in a cheap edition by Swan Sonnenschein in 1887, and eventually his other novels appeared: *Love Among the Artists* in 1900 and *The Irrational Knot* in 1905. Only *Immaturity*, rejected by every publisher who saw it on both sides of the Atlantic, remained unpublished—until 1930.

Shaw added an appendix to a second edition of *An Unsocial Socialist* in 1887 in which his hero advises the author to give up novel writing. This advice Shaw took.

He became disenchanted with the novel form (abandoning a sixth opus) and was to find his metier as a playwright. From his first play produced in 1892, *Widowers' Houses*, he went on to become the great dramatist of the century, producing more than fifty plays over a period of nearly sixty years. Among the best known are *Arms and the Man, Candida, Mrs. Warren's Profession, The Devil's Disciple, Caesar and Cleopatra, Captain Brassbound's Conversion, Man and Superman, Major Barbara, Pygmalion, Heartbreak House, Saint Joan*. And he went on to win the Nobel Prize for literature.

And when he no longer needed them, the publishers clamored for any piece of writing with his name on it. But let us allow George Bernard Shaw to have the last word on publishers:

I object to publishers: the one service they have done me is to teach me to do without them. They combine commercial rascality with artistic touchiness and pettishness, without being either good business men or fine judges of literature. All that is necessary to the production of a book is an author and a bookseller, without any intermediate parasite.

JOHN STEINBECK

"Not for us—"

As if further evidence is needed, John Steinbeck's rise to the top also serves to illustrate the compulsive devotion in the face of harsh rejection that is intrinsic to all creative writers. One of the best known and most popular of American novelists, Steinbeck began his career, like most aspiring writers, by collecting rejection slips in the struggle toward acceptance.

Born in 1902 in Salinas, California, John Steinbeck entered Stanford University in 1919, insisting he would be a writer. He attended intermittently for the next six years, leaving finally without a degree. But his two stories which appeared in the *Stanford Spectator* in 1924 may be considered his first published pieces.

He left his native state when his early attempts at writing were unsuccessful. One article on his treks around California elicited this comment from the editor of the Monterey newspaper to whom he had sent it: "Not for us—it'll turn away the tourists." Steinbeck nevertheless continued writing stories of the Monterey working people and descriptions of the wondrous Monterey scenery before leaving in 1925 to try to establish himself as an author in the literary capital of the country.

In New York he again failed to achieve recognition as a writer. Impoverished, he managed to get a job laboring, not at his writing, but with barrows of cement in the construction of Madison Square Garden. He managed also to get a job as a reporter but achieved neither satisfaction nor success. Good luck eluded him again even when the stories he wrote appealed to Guy Holt, an editor at the publishing firm of Robert M. McBride & Company. Holt requested an additional six stories to make up a viable book for publication. Within six weeks Steinbeck delivered a manuscript of nine stories to the editor's office, only to be told that Guy Holt had left for another publishing house and that McBride, finding the stories below their standards, was not obliged to honor the commitment. He took the manuscript to Holt at his new firm, only to be told that the John Day Company would not publish stories by an unknown writer. Penniless and with no prospects, he returned to California. Although New York had beaten him, when he next returned some ten years later, he was a literary celebrity.

Back in California he wrote novels and stories which were unsalable. Two early novels he discarded. A third failed to find a publisher. His first piece of writing to earn money was a short story called "The Gifts of Iban" written under a pseudonym in 1927. His first novel, *Cup of Gold*, he wrote and rewrote until its satisfactory completion in January 1928. His mentors encouraged him to send it to New York—where it received a round of rejections.

Among seven publishing houses to reject *Cup of Gold* were Farrar and Rinehart, Scribner's, and Harper Brothers. Finally, the eighth submission brought an acceptance, ironically from McBride, the house that had rejected his stories two years earlier. John Steinbeck's first published novel, a fictional biography of a seventeenth-century Caribbean pirate (with the revealing subtitle of "A Life of Sir

Henry Morgan, Buccaneer, with Occasional Reference to History") appeared in August 1929.

However, *Cup of Gold* was no guarantee that success would follow. In 1930, McBride rejected his second novel, *To A God Unknown*, and further rejections came from Harper Brothers and Farrar and Rinehart and what seemed like every publisher in New York before it finally appeared in 1933. In 1932 the publishing firm of William Morris rejected *The Pastures of Heaven*, a collection of ten stories set in a California valley. It continued to make the rounds as did the manuscript of *To a God Unknown*, which his new agent was unable to place. But on the 27th of February 1932, his thirtieth birthday, came the good news that the prestigious British firm of Jonathan Cape Ltd. and Harrison Smith, its American subsidiary, would take on *The Pastures of Heaven*. So enthusiastic was the Cape and Smith editor, Robert Ballou, that he offered contracts on Steinbeck's next two novels. Steinbeck began rewriting *To a God Unknown*.

Then followed the bad news. Cape and Smith, riddled with financial problems, was reorganized and Ballou left. His new firm of Brewer, Warren and Putnam assumed Steinbeck's contract. But they too were struggling with economic hardships due to the Great Depression and were unable to produce *To a God Unknown*. Robert Ballou formed his own publishing firm, Robert O. Ballou and Company, and loyally undertook to publish it under his own imprint. While Ballou was also floundering in the Depression environment, the manuscript went to half a dozen others. Simon and Schuster expressed interest before Ballou managed to extricate himself from business difficulties. Now it was Steinbeck's turn to be loyal, and he stayed with Ballou. Delayed until November 1933, the book sold less than a thousand copies and caused few ripples on the literary scene

Literary waters did ripple when, after a number of rejections, two stories that became the first two parts of *The Red Pony* appeared in November and December 1933 in a major literary journal, *The North American Review.* Steinbeck began writing stories of the poor Mexicans—*paisanos*—who lived in a shantytown above Monterey known as Tortilla Flat. But without a commercial success yet to his name, he had trouble placing his fourth book. Of his first three, fewer than three thousand copies had been sold by 1935, the year that marks the turning point and Steinbeck's firm placement on the road to fame and fortune.

He finished *Tortilla Flat* in March 1934, but even his agent, Mavis McIntosh, was unimpressed. Ballou shrank from *Tortilla Flat* because of his company's precarious financial condition (due in no small part to the unprofitable publication of *To a God Unknown*). Furthermore, he did not like the new novel. It was "too slight" and "it didn't make sense." He turned it down declaring that "it isn't an important book and it doesn't add to your stature as a novelist."

Neither did several other publishers like the story that was deemed too trivial in the difficult Depression era. Knopf was among those who rejected *Tortilla Flat*, and the note written by Louis Kronenberger expressed regret that he could not foresee its success but added, "I think the man has a future."

Steinbeck consoled himself by writing short stories that eventually appeared in *The Long Valley* in 1939, and he began a protest volume about the plight of migrant workers and a strike in an orchard valley that became *In Dubious Battle.*

Nine times was *Tortilla Flat* rejected before fate stepped in, in the form of Pascal Covici, to establish Steinbeck as an important writer who did indeed have a future. By chance, a bookseller in Chicago and an advocate of Steinbeck's work, commended the author to the head of the small New York publishing house of Covici-Friede, who happened to be visiting the Argus Book Shop. He induced Pascal Covici to read a remaindered copy of *The Pastures of Heaven*. Covici was equally impressed and requested further works. With the manuscript of *Tortilla Flat* available, Covici was delighted to become the publisher of Steinbeck's fourth novel after making an offer in January 1935 that could not be refused. He would publish not only *Tortilla Flat* and all future works but would also reissue previous works.

Tortilla Flat, published on 28 May 1935, was the turning point. It became known throughout the country by July and created a demand for the works of Steinbeck. Hollywood bought the film rights. No longer would he lack for money or fame. It marked the end to Steinbeck's struggle with poverty and the start of a prosperous future in a literary career.

He completed *In Dubious Battle* in January 1935, but it seemed that Covici backed out of the agreement when a letter of rejection arrived from Harry Black, an editor at Covici-Friede and a Marxist, who disliked it. "The book is totally inaccurate," he wrote. "It is sure to offend people on the right as well as on the left." But other publishers wanted the novel now that Steinbeck's name was a marketable commodity. The manuscript was sent to Bobbs-Merrill and promptly accepted. Meanwhile, Pat Covici returned from his out-of-town trip and discovered what had occurred in his absence. He dismissed the meddling editor on the spot, apologized to Steinbeck, and asked for the return of the novel. Steinbeck had a choice and chose to remain with Covici.

No, his road to publication was not smooth. He fumed in a letter: "I have worked for so long against opposition, first of my parents who wanted me to be a lawyer and then of publishers who want me to be anything but a writer, that I work well under opposition."

Covici's business failed in 1938, but Steinbeck remained loyal to his discoverer and followed him when Covici became an executive editor for the Viking Press. The professional and personal friendship lasted all their lives. *Of Mice and Men* became an immediate best seller when it appeared early in 1937, while *The Grapes of Wrath* precipitated an avalanche of acclaim and became the top seller of 1939 and the Pulitzer Prize winner. From the time of its appearance in an edition of 19,804 copies it has never been out of print and has never sold less than 50,000 copies a year in the United States.

Among the massive oeuvre of Steinbeck novels are *The Moon Is Down* (1942), *Cannery Row* (1945), *The Wayward Bus* (1947), *The Pearl* (1947), *The Red Pony* (1945), *East of Eden* (1952), *Sweet Thursday* (1954), and *The Winter of Our Discontent* (1961). He was awarded the Nobel Prize for literature in December 1962, a half dozen years before his death on 20 December 1968. The mind recoils from contemplation of how things might have gone if Steinbeck had not "worked for so long against opposition. . . of publishers who want me to be anything but a writer."

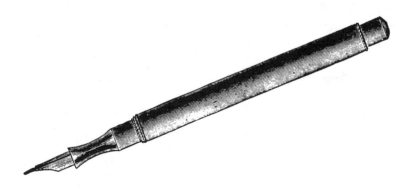

HARRIET BEECHER STOWE

*A novel by a woman on an unpopular and
controversial subject was too great a risk.*

Such was the impact of *Uncle Tom's Cabin* that when
President Abraham Lincoln met its author at the White House
in 1862, he is said to have greeted her with the words, "So
you're the little woman who wrote the book that started this
great war!"

Yet, the little woman had begun the writing career that
culminated in her masterpiece on slavery when, as a married
woman with children, she decided not to be a slave to
domestic chores. By earning money with her writing, she was
able to hire servants to help with the housework and the
children so that she could write three hours a day. The
formula was successful, and her stories and sketches
appeared in magazines; her literary efforts began to produce
monetary rewards by 1838.

Her writing career began when she left the East, where
she was born on 14 June 1811, in Connecticut, when her
father moved his evangelical Christian crusade to Cincinnati.
There her sister Catharine, eleven years older, founded a
school. Harriet taught and wrote children's text books. There
she married Calvin Stowe and began to have children in quick
succession—seven, but one died in infancy. There too, in
Cincinnati, she had her apprenticeship as a writer.

Her short pieces were so successful that in 1842 Harper Brothers of Boston sought her out to discuss the possibility of bringing out a volume of her collected short stories. In April she left for Boston, staying until September. Her destiny as a literary woman was being molded. One letter home to her husband made a request that intriguingly precedes by nearly a century one of Virginia Woolf's injunctions: "If I am to write, I must have a room to myself, which shall be *my* room."

Her collection of fifteen stories and sketches appeared in 1843 carrying the unwieldy title, *The Mayflower; or, Sketches of Scenes and Characters among the Descendants of the Pilgrims.*

She was on the way to becoming one of the most popular and best paid authors of the nineteenth century. A sketch published in January 1845, "Immediate Emancipation," was based on a true story and contained the ideas which later brought international fame. It used dialogue, plot, and an attack on the institution of slavery that became the germ of her masterpiece.

Her lengthy novel, *Uncle Tom's Cabin*, ran first in weekly installments in the *National Era*, from 5 June 1851 to 1 April 1852. She had been offered $300 for a story which was originally to have three or four installments but grew to become forty. So busy was she while *Uncle Tom* was being serialized, that she missed deadlines. Among other things, she was involved yet again with yet another school founded by her sister Catharine, who was eager to have *Uncle Tom* out of the way so that Harriet could devote her attention to the new educational venture.

Catharine, like many of the other family members, was also a writer. She took Harriet's manuscript to her own publisher, Phillips, Sampson & Company of Boston, and offered them the powerful novel. In view of the enormous popularity of the *Uncle Tom* series, it must have been a great shock to have the book refused; but refused it was, on the grounds that an antislavery novel would not sell even a thousand copies and would damage the firm's business in the South. The publisher's rejection expressed serious concerns and fears that producing a novel by a woman on such a controversial subject was too great a risk to undertake. What if it were written by a man, one wonders? Or had nothing of import to say on any subject? In any case, how could they have ignored public response to the serialization! They declined and in so doing, declined a masterpiece and a fortune.

Of the tens of thousands of readers, Mrs. Jewett was one typical reader who was moved to tears by *Uncle Tom's Cabin* in the pages of the *National Era*. Perhaps her steady urging that her husband solicit Mrs. Stowe's story in book form for his small publishing house was not a factor in its acceptance, but it was certainly indicative of the vast and positive public response. John P. Jewett (who had already published books by other family members) did not specialize in fiction, but he decided to gamble on its publication.

Jewett's acceptance was not without misgivings. He had agreed to produce it when only a third of the story was written and had anticipated a slim volume at a low price. As the serial increased in length, he became alarmed. His resources were scant, and he pleaded with the writer to terminate the unpopular subject that would be unsuccessful in two volumes. Any misgivings he had ceased immediately upon publication.

On 20 March 1852, John P. Jewett released the novel that sold three thousand copies the first day, ten thousand copies the first week, and three hundred thousand within the first year. With a contract giving her ten per cent of sales, Harriet Beecher Stowe received ten thousand dollars within three months, "the largest sum of money ever received by an author, either American or European, from the sale of a single work in so short a period of time," the New York *Daily Times* noted. In Britain, sales figures were triple the astounding United States figures.

The rest of the story of the literary classic that has never been out of print is, as they say, history. Harriet Beecher Stowe produced a second antislavery novel in 1856, *Dred: A Tale of the Great Dismal Swamp*. But nothing she wrote ever equaled the sensational effect of her magnum opus. She continued to write, lecture, and care for her large family, until her death on 1 July 1896 at the age of eighty-five. One may well part from the history of *Uncle Tom's Cabin* wondering what Phillips, Sampson & Company thought of their decision to forego the opportunity of being the publisher of that great masterpiece.

JULES VERNE

"You took on an impossible task, and you
did not pull it off. Nobody will ever
believe your prophecies."

As a student in Paris, Jules Verne developed a strong
attachment to the theatre and struggled to make a living from
it. His mother sent care packages of food from Nantes (where
he was born in 1828) and helped with his laundry, while his
father tried to convince him to join the family law practice. But
Verne gave up law in deference to his passion for the theatre.
He wrote plays, as well as short stories, and worked at the
Theatre Lyrique with Alexander Dumas from 1851 to 1856.

Nevertheless, his dream of becoming an important
Parisian dramatist never materialized. He wrote some fifteen
plays between 1851 and 1863, nine of which were never
produced. He tried his pen at stories and travel literature, but
his *Voyage in Ecosse,* emanating from a trip he took to
Edinburgh in 1859, was never published. He did achieve
a modicum of success with two novellas, *The Mutineers,*
first published in 1851 in an illustrated family magazine,
and *Martin Paz,* the following year. But, finding himself
unsuccessful as a man of the theatre, he took another literary
route to fame and fortune. At twenty-six, Verne left the theatre
struggle to devote himself to a struggle with literature.

Intrigued with balloons, and inspired by Edgar Allan Poe, Verne wrote an account of a balloon flight across central Africa. The editor of the *Revue des Deux Mondes* was willing to print it but unwilling to pay anything more than the honor and prestige that would accrue to the unknown writer.

Verne was accustomed to rebuffs from publishers and had in the past consigned his manuscripts to the flames in despair. Fortunately, he now took his history of ballooning to the man who was to become his publisher and friend, Pierre-Jules Hetzel. Hetzel advised him to novelize it; and the result was *Five Weeks in a Balloon,* an instant best seller and the turning point in his life. The year was 1863 and he was thirty-six. Verne had found a publisher and Hetzel had found a genius, a genius who went on writing brilliantly in the science fiction genre.

The following year Verne produced another classic, *Voyage to the Center of the Earth. Twenty Thousand Leagues under the Sea* appeared in 1873, and when he was over forty, he enjoyed the greatest fiction success of his lifetime, *Around the World in Eighty Days* (1874). By the time he wrote *The Mysterious Island* (1875), he was at the peak of his career and universally famous. He was seventy-eight when he died in 1905, leaving a legacy of over sixty novels filled with imaginary adventures that continue to delight.

The world-famous figure continues to fascinate generations with his amazing adventures. He is today among the most translated authors of all time with over twenty-five million copies printed in forty different languages. But in his own time he continued to experience publishers' rejections despite an outstanding writing career. *Paris in the Twentieth Century,* written in 1863, looked into the future and depicted a world filled with cars and traffic jams. It prophesied the electric chair (actually invented in the United States twenty-five years later) to replace the guillotine. It conjured up the fax machine and the telephone. And it described some of the horrific consequences of modern technology.

When Hetzel saw *Paris in the Twentieth Century* in the nineteenth century, he advised Verne to abandon it: "You took on an impossible task, and you did not pull it off. Nobody will ever believe your prophecies."

Verne, too busy writing some sixty other novels, dutifully abandoned this one. It remained unpublished and forgotten in its place in a one-ton safe. Assumed destroyed during World War II, the manuscript was recently uncovered and published in 1994 in France by Hachette/Le Cherche Midi—just one hundred thirty-one years after its initial rejection by the publisher.

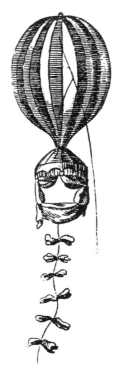

EVELYN WAUGH

His first novel was refused on the
grounds of indelicacy.

Being born into a home life that was a world of books, with a
father who was a publisher and an older brother who became
an editor and author, Evelyn Waugh would seem to be a
candidate for easy publication. However, despite easy access
to such influential contacts, he was to feel a bit of the
heartbreak of rejection.

His twenty-first birthday, 28 October 1924, found him
unsettled and unsure of himself. He had left Oxford without
completing a degree, and his prospects were poor. He tried a
variety of occupations including painting, printing, and
newspaper work. He took several teaching positions, first in
Wales, then in Aston Clinton. He dabbled in writing and
destroyed an unfinished novel, *The Temple of Thatch*, when a
trusted friend could not extol its literary merits. One long
story, *The Balance*, he sent to Leonard Woolf at the Hogarth
Press. Woolf returned it, as did a literary agent to whom
Waugh had also sent a copy. He tried other publishers
unsuccessfully, including Arrowsmith, before giving it up.

In the spring of 1926 his brother Alec, an editor at
Chapman and Hall was in search of contributions for the
Georgian Stories which he was then editing. He saw *The
Balance*, liked it, and agreed to include Evelyn's piece for

publication the following October. It was no small achievement for a fledgling and unknown author.

Noah; or the Future of Intoxication, was the title of another idea that he proposed in October 1926 to Kegan Paul, the publishers of the *Today and Tomorrow* series of short books. They welcomed the idea but rejected the actual story.

When Michael Sadleir, recognizing the originality of *The Balance*, requested a story for *The New Decameron*, Evelyn produced "The Tutor's Tale. A House of Gentlefolks" and was pleased to have the story accepted in March 1927. It was published later that year—another success.

Introduced to the firm of Duckworth by his Oxford friend Anthony Powell, Waugh was commissioned by the publisher to write a biography of the Pre-Raphaelite painter Dante Gabriel Rossetti to coincide with the centenary of the artist's birth the following year. An advance of £50 helped to relieve Waugh's pecuniary needs. In the spring of 1928 appeared *Rossetti: His Life and Works*, an accomplished study that marked the end of his writing apprenticeship.

As the publisher of *Rossetti*, Duckworth was the natural recipient of Waugh's next book, *Decline and Fall*. But Duckworth declined the novel, and Waugh fell into a rage. The publisher was shocked by the novel's salaciousness and remained sensitive to the possibility of lawsuits. Waugh understood and accepted that his text might have to be restrained but was angered by the excessive alterations and deletions which substantially changed the novel. Even the vaguest suggestion of sex had to be excised. The hero's running about without trousers required modification. But Gerald Duckworth's decision must have been exacerbated by his sympathy with Lady Burghclere, a distant relation, who strongly opposed her daughter's recent marriage to Evelyn Waugh.

Waugh would have preferred independence from family and friends, but his marriage to Evelyn Gardner (who was to become known as She-Evelyn) placed him in financial straits with no time to send the manuscript off and await responses. Immediate publication was urgent. He took it to the firm of which his father was managing director, Chapman and Hall. Fortunately, his father was abroad. The board members reached a stalemate on whether to take it on, and the final vote in its favor was made by R. E. Neale of the technical department, not by Waugh's father or brother.

Chapman and Hall made several suggestions to purify the novel for publication. For example, it would be more seemly for the Station Master to seek employment for his sister-in-law rather than for his sister. And lavatories should be altered to become boiler-rooms. The year of publication, also the year of his marriage, was 1928.

The book was an immediate success but his marriage was not, breaking up after a year. Waugh went on to become a hugely successful novelist. Between *Decline and Fall* at the age of twenty-four and his death at sixty-three, he produced an additional sixteen novels—including *Vile Bodies* (1930), *Black Mischief* (1932), *A Handful of Dust* (1934), *Brideshead Revisited* (1945), and *The Ordeal of Gilbert Pinfold* (1957)—as well as short stories, travel books, and journalism.

A new edition of *Decline and Fall* published in 1962 contained a Preface by the author discussing the rejection thirty-three years earlier on the grounds of indelicacy. By 1962, Evelyn Waugh was secure enough in his literary reputation—and so was the publisher—to revert to the original.

H. G. WELLS

"... would be exceedingly distasteful to
the public which buys books published
by our firm."

If Sarah Wells had her way, her son might have become
an insignificant but respectable draper instead of the well-
known author of such volumes as *The Time Machine* (1895),
The Invisible Man (1897), *The War of the Worlds* (1898), and
Kipps (1905).

Herbert George Wells was born in 1866 in Bromley in
Kent, the son of a struggling shopkeeper, but spent crucial
years at the great country house in Sussex known as Up Park.
After his father's business failed when the lad was eleven, his
mother, a former lady's maid, returned to work as housekeeper at Up Park. The grand place opened vistas for Wells. It
was there that he read books from the well-stocked library
and first began writing. He produced a gossip sheet called *The
Up Park Alarmist* at Christmas 1880. About seven years later
he returned from London to recuperate from illness; the
invalid read voraciously, and his reading taught him the basic
principles of writing. "The place had a great effect upon me,"
he wrote in his autobiography. Now owned and maintained by
the National Trust, Uppark (as the name has been updated) is
open to the public who come also to pay tribute to the author

who described the house as Bladesover in *Tono-Bungay* and whose compulsion to write was first exhibited here.

Although he showed great intelligence and much promise, his mother saw no value in furthering his education and encouraged his apprenticeship as a draper's assistant. Fortunately, the man who was to become a literary giant was more ambitious for himself and broke out of several detested apprenticeships for the sake of furthering his education. He attended Midhurst Grammar School and managed to secure a scholarship in 1884 to the Normal School of Science in Kensington (now part of London University), where he studied biology with T. H. Huxley. After graduating in 1890, he held several teaching posts and wrote scientific articles, beginning his literary career as an insignificant Grub Street journalist. He began publishing numerous articles in a variety of periodicals, most notably the *Pall Mall Gazette* and the *Saturday Review*, and began earning a good living. By 1893 his income from writing definitely allowed him to adopt the profession of letters. That year he also wrote his first book-length publication, *A Textbook of Biology.*

Commissioned to write a serial story for *The New Review*, Wells put his ideas into fictional form in *The Time Machine*, perhaps his most famous book. Published by Heinemann in 1895, *The Time Machine* was a triumph that has never been out of print since its first edition. Other books soon followed this pioneering work of English science fiction: *The Island of Dr. Moreau* (1896), *The Invisible Man* (1897), *The War of the Worlds* (1898), and *When the Sleeper Wakes* (1899). His career had taken off.

He went on to write novels about the ordinary man such as *Love and Mr. Lewisham* (1900), *Kipps: The Story of a Simple Soul* (1905), *Tono-Bungay* (1909) and *The History of Mr. Polly* (1910). He depicted with humor the revolt of ordinary men who escape from society's traps. Later novels tend to focus on ideas and have been criticized as tedious. His final novel, *You Can't Be Too Careful*, contains much social preaching, the very flaw that Virginia Woolf argued against, maintaining that a good novel ought to express character rather than doctrine. Most of his vast output of books consisted not of fiction but of works of science, philosophy, politics, economics, history. In particular, *The Outline of History* (1920) met with a hugely enthusiastic response and made him wealthy.

His entrance into the profession was not the depressingly familiar one, fraught with rejection, but a relatively easy acceptance. He was himself aware that he had arrived with comparative ease: "Earning a living by writing is a frightful gamble," he wrote in 1919. "I have been lucky but it took me eight years, while I was teaching & then doing anxious journalism, to get established upon a comfortably paying footing."

Oddly enough, he was at a peak in his career when rejection came. He sent his manuscript of *Ann Veronica,* the story of an emancipated woman, to Macmillan at the end of September 1908. On 16 October Frederick Macmillan refused publication on the grounds that the plot developed "on lines that would be exceedingly distasteful to the public which buys books published by our firm." Fearful of scandal, Macmillan took the step of turning it down despite the realization that it would mean the end of the contract with a literary lion. Their refusal remains a mystery as the eponymous lady is as uninhibited as the lady in *Tono-Bungay,* which they did accept. *Ann Veronica* went to Fisher Unwin and appeared in 1909. A shocking book for its time, the novel became a great success. It is still in print and widely read, particularly by those interested in feminist studies.

The New Machiavelli also struggled to emerge in print. Wells offered the "large and outspoken" book about politics to Sir Frederick Macmillan in October 1909. Eager to get Wells back, the publisher offered a contract without bothering to read any of it until late June. What he read shocked him. Wells tried to revise it to suit Macmillan but did not succeed. Macmillan offered only the hope that Heinemann would take over and helped him to find a publisher.

But neither Heinemann nor Chapman and Hall were willing. Wells went directly to William Heinemann, who told him that although it was "certainly one of the most brilliant books I have read for years and one which has given me the greatest possible pleasure in reading" he could not risk a novel "so charged with a dangerous (and perhaps libelous) atmosphere." He worried about characters who were identifiable as Beatrice and Sidney Webb. Furthermore, he felt that Wells was too demanding about terms of the contract. After months of haggling and searching, Macmillan found a willing publisher in John Lane, who issued it in 1911.

Wells also experienced some difficulty in having his work placed from the early 1930s, when he was getting bad press. His case offers evidence that a secure place in the literary world does not insure a passport to publication. Rejection can come—and frequently does—at any time in a writer's career.

His output was enormous. Of at least 156 books that he wrote, some are imaginative and extraordinary, some are controversial and offensive. But his worldwide influence is unquestionable. His last book, *Mind at the End of Its Tether*, appeared fifty years after his first and expressed gloom about the future of man. His own future lasted another year. Wells died on 13 August 1946, just weeks before his eightieth birthday. It seems appropriate to quote the words of J.B. Priestley delivered in an address at the funeral of H. G. Wells: "His literary genius was rich and rare—the best of his novels and short stories are among the finest creations of our time—but he belongs not only to English literature, but also to world history."

OSCAR WILDE

He exploited eccentricity to achieve
publication.

A study of Oscar Wilde's triumphant entry into literary fame
does not yield a formula that can be easily adopted by many,
for he went to enormous extremes to gain acceptance by the
public in order to be accepted for publication.

Born Oscar Fingal O'Flahertie Wills Wilde on 16 October
1854, he shortened the cumbersome name as soon as he
could reasonably do so, as he explained to a friend, to insure
easy flow of "a name which is destined to be in everybody's
mouth." A study of his life reveals his progress toward fulfill-
ment of the ambition to be famous.

He loved life with an irrepressible boyish exuberance
which predestined him to become a victim of the selfish and
dissipated Lord Alfred Douglas, with whom he became
infatuated. With Lord Alfred, he entered into an illicit and
seedy homosexual world and became involved in disputes
with his friend's father, the unscrupulous, despicable, and
corrupt Marquis of Queensberry, who brought about Wilde's
downfall.

But before the sordid events which led to Wilde's
imprisonment and exile, life was wonderful. At Oxford, he
was a popular student and good scholar with a great love of
poetry as well as a writer of poems, several of which appeared

in magazines. In his last year as an undergraduate in 1878, he won the coveted Newdigate Prize for his poem, *Ravenna*, and prophesied to a friend: "I'll be a poet, a writer, a dramatist. Somehow or other I'll be famous, and if not famous I'll be notorious."

His ascent to fame began in London. With high spirits and a love of fun, full of charm and wit, he made his mark in society by posing before the public. His eccentric manner of dress caused him to be identified as the leader of the aesthetic or pre-Raphaelite movement, a role in which he reveled.

Fame engulfed him through a fortunate accident—Gilbert and Sullivan's *Patience* of 1881, a satiric opera that dealt with aestheticism. People came to believe that the character of Reginald Bunthorne, the fleshly poet who walked down Piccadilly with a poppy or a lily in his medieval hand, was based on Wilde. Eager for celebrity, he encouraged that impression, basking in the limelight thrust upon him. Of that phenomenon he said: "Anyone could have done that. The great and difficult thing was what I achieved—to make the whole world believe that I had done it."

Caricatured, satirized, and lionized, Wilde now considered the time propitious for bringing forward his volume of poems for publication. Apparently, he had earlier tried publisher after publisher, to no avail. He explained to a friend that he had entered the aesthetic phase explicitly to become a known quantity and thus insure being published. It would seem that his scheme paid off, for *Poems* appeared in a luxurious edition in 1881. But. . . .

But the fact is that Wilde paid the total cost of production himself. Even after achieving a high level of publicity, and despite his prominence in social circles, Wilde could find no publisher to take it on. The luxurious volume was issued by David Bogue, who received ten per cent commission. Reviews were unfavorable. A presentation copy sent to the Oxford

Debating Society was deemed unacceptable and rudely returned to the author.

If a volume of verse could not yield financial success, a play might, Wilde reasoned, and wrote *Vera* in 1880. Again he had it printed at his own expense. Again critics dismissed it, not recognizing the qualities which were soon to make the author famous as a dramatist. Indeed, the typical Wildean epigram is already present in his first play—spoken by the Czar's Prime Minister: "Experience, the name men give to their mistakes"—and recast in *Lady Windermere's Fan*.

Despite his experience, Wilde made another mistake with a blank verse tragedy called *The Duchess of Padua*. Mary Anderson backed it, but the publisher hacked it. The reason for refusal may remain forever unknown, for after Wilde read the answer, he unemotionally tore off a bit of the blue rejection notice, crumpled it into a pellet, and placed it in his mouth apparently swallowing the unfavorable verdict. Wilde admitted at the end of his life that *The Duchess* was "unfit for publication—the only one of my works that comes under that category."

Not until a decade after his initial publishing fiasco, did Wilde begin producing his great works: *The Picture of Dorian Gray* (1891) and *Lady Windermere's Fan* (1892), followed by *Salome, A Woman of No Importance, An Ideal Husband*. His career peaked in 1895 with his masterpiece, *The Importance of Being Earnest*.

In the light of such greatness, it is all too easy to forget the difficulties that Wilde encountered when first he sought to be a published author. To an American customs officer, he had announced that he had nothing to declare but his genius. Indeed, his genius, unrecognized in early attempts at publication, survives and continues to declare itself in the great works he created.

THOMAS WOLFE

"It is so long—so terribly long—that it is
most difficult for a reader to sustain
interest to the end. . . and so much of it
has been done, and so often, that we
hesitate to take another chance."

The story of Thomas Wolfe's rise to success as an author is
an ordinary one, full of struggles and disappointments and
eventual good luck. Wolfe's good fortune arrived when he
came to the attention of a great genius in American publishing
history, Maxwell Evarts Perkins.

In his capacity as an editor with the firm of Charles
Scribner's Sons for thirty-six years, Max Perkins was totally
devoted to discovering promising young writers. He discovered, and guided to full fruition, such great talents as
F. Scott Fitzgerald and Ernest Hemingway, as well as Thomas
Wolfe. He fought against the establishment for publication of
these unconventional writers, putting his own career on the
line, and his battles and exertions contributed to a revo-
lutionary new American literature. It was due to his efforts
that Thomas Wolfe achieved a permanent place in literary
history with influential and lasting works from his first novel
to his last, from *Look Homeward, Angel* to *You Can't Go
Home Again*.

After Thomas Wolfe left North Carolina, where he was born in Asheville on 3 October 1900, he studied playwriting at Harvard University and received a Master's degree in 1922. To support himself, he accepted a position at the Washington Square division of New York University where he taught English composition intermittently from 1924 to 1930, happily giving up the position when publication of his first novel allowed him to feel secure enough to devote himself entirely to writing.

He went to Europe in 1924 to gain experience and to write. On the journey home, he met Aline Bernstein, a married woman of forty-four, small and vivacious, with a successful career in stage and costume design, and Jewish. He was an eager youth of nearly twenty-five, over six feet tall, with career frustrations, and anti-Semitic. The combination was explosive, but Aline brought him love and friendship, finances and connections. Her influence helped him initially to step from apprenticeship status to recognition as a successful and famous figure in the literary world.

By the age of twenty-eight, Wolfe had written three plays, a novel, a travel journal, and numerous stories and sketches—but had published next to nothing. Only student contributions to university magazines had appeared in print as well as a brief excerpt from his travel notes ("London Tower") in the Asheville *Citizen*. Nevertheless, he began a second novel, knowing that it was his destiny to be a writer. While a student at Harvard he had written in a letter to his mother, "I intend to wreak out my soul on paper and express it all."

He struggled and wreaked out his soul with the writing of his first novel, *O Lost*, finally completing it in March 1928. Aline Bernstein, his patron and mistress, knew the managing editor and took it to Boni & Liveright, a young firm known for publishing unconventional new writers. They kept it for five weeks before declining to publish what they considered to be merely another "autobiography of a young man—and so much of it has been done, and so often, that we hesitate to take another chance. . ." Furthermore, they objected, "It is so long—so terribly long—that it is most difficult for a reader to sustain an interest to the end." Rejected, Wolfe later enjoyed the satisfaction of revenge when he satirized the firm as Rawng & Wright in a novel in which the protagonist castigates them for not knowing how to read books, just how to publish them.

Aline had another friend with a connection at Harcourt, Brace, but the manuscript received another rejection. Then another friend, a literary agent, sent it to Longmans, Green & Company where it was again rejected. And Covici-Friede added its name to the list of refusals, denouncing it as "a semi-autobiographical novel of over 250,000 words . . . fearfully diffuse . . . marred by stylistic clichés, outlandish adjectives and similes, etc." but nevertheless asking for an option on Wolfe's next book.

At last came a positive response. Wolfe was again in Europe when Maxwell Perkins sent a letter expressing interest and inviting him to visit Scribners on his return. Wolfe, having received enough rejections to know the bitter taste of disappointment, knew better than to drop everything and rush home to face the possible pain of yet another rejection.

But Perkins saw its power and was willing to help him cut and revise the gigantic and sprawling manuscript which nobody else wanted. He worked desperately to eliminate extraneous segments and arrange the material—a record of the ancestry, birth, childhood, and youth of Eugene Gant—until eventually the eleven hundred typewritten pages were reduced to eight hundred. The problem of cutting and condensing plagued Wolfe all his life. Perkins also requested a better title. Wolfe complied by extracting a three-word phrase from a line in Milton's *Lycidas.*

Look Homeward, Angel was published in October 1929, and Wolfe received the first copy of his first published book on his twenty-ninth birthday. He recognized the large share Aline played in the realization of his first novel and dedicated it to her but nevertheless was ready to break up the relationship soon after publication, which brought him substantial success and represented a turning point in his life. Thomas Wolfe was launched as a writer and literary celebrity. The book was highly praised and brought him acclaim from all parts except his hometown of Asheville, where residents recognized themselves with all their failings revealed. Awarded a $2500 Guggenheim fellowship in March, he again went abroad where he could be financially secure and work hard, isolated and undisturbed, on his next novel.

He returned with a vast amount of notes rather than with a completed book. While difficulties with the novel continued, he managed to produce a story called "A Portrait of Bascom Hawke" that was accepted for publication in the April 1932 issue of *Scribner's Magazine* and won a prize in a short novel competition.

He then lunged into the writing of a book called *K-19,* the number of the Pullman car that ran between Asheville and New York City, working frantically on it in the spring of 1932. Perkins was equally enthusiastic—until he read it. He rejected it as not good enough to follow *Look Homeward, Angel.* And Wolfe submissively accepted the rebuff knowing that most segments of the manuscript would find their way into future books.

Wolfe's second book finally appeared in 1935. *Of Time and the River* continued the Eugene Gant chronicle from his leaving Harvard to his meeting Esther Jack (the fictional counterpart of Aline Bernstein) on the return voyage to

America. It was dedicated to Perkins citing his patience, help, friendship. Also published that year was a book of short stories, *From Death to Morning*. *The Story of a Novel* (1936)—originally a lecture given at a writers' conference in Boulder, Colorado—was the story and critical explanation of how *Of Time and the River* had been written.

But the friendship with Perkins deteriorated. Among a number of reasons for the ultimate break with his editor was a virulent attack by Bernard De Voto accusing the author of retaining too much "placental" matter and having his novels put together by "Mr. Perkins and the assembly-line at Scribners." Wolfe needed to prove his literary independence.

In the summer of 1937 he went home again to Asheville to a rented cabin in the woods to ponder his relationship with his editor and to write in solitude. He produced stories to keep himself financially independent. "The Child by Tiger" had trouble finding a place; it was too daring for *Collier's* readers and was turned down also by *Redbook* before being accepted by the *Saturday Evening Post*.

"Chickamauga" he considered one of the best pieces he had ever written. Yet, despite the name he had built up for himself and despite the fact that it had recently printed another of his stories ("The Child by Tiger"), the *Saturday Evening Post* rejected this one on the grounds that it had insufficient "story element." The *American Mercury* also rejected the story that eventually appeared in the *Yale Review*. Other stories appeared in other magazines. And Wolfe, after agonizing for two years, made the decision to leave Scribners. He courted other publishers until he ultimately settled for Harper & Brothers.

By 1938 Thomas Wolfe was dead. He had fallen ill in July while on holiday in the West. Pneumonia had opened up and released into his bloodstream an old tubercular lesion in his lung. He was moved to Johns Hopkins Hospital for an operation which revealed incurable miliary tuberculosis of the brain. His short and troubled life ended on 15 September, just eighteen days before his thirty-eighth birthday. The brief literary career had lasted just nine years. *The Web and the Rock* (1939) was published posthumously, as was its sequel and last major novel, *You Can't Go Home Again* (1940).

ZANE GREY

"I don't see anything in this to convince
me you can write either narrative or
fiction."

Zane Grey may not be considered by many the ultimate,
either alphabetically or critically, but his simple rise to fame
as a writer may serve as a summary of so many typical
publishing stories.

He was born in Zanesville, Ohio, on 31 January 1875 and
given the unfortunate name of Pearl for no clear reason. His
first manuscript was destroyed by his father, burned when the
young lad of fourteen was caught stealing chickens with his
mischievous gang of friends, all members of a secret club.

Perhaps he was trying to prove his manhood and
counteract his effeminate name by becoming the organizer of
a group of vandals who indulged in wanton acts of destruction:
breaking windows, invading empty houses, uprooting tulip
beds, stealing melons from fields and hens from roosts. In one
all-night secret session, in a secret cave, he read aloud to
his cohorts "Jim of the Cave," a story he had written on
the reverse side of strips of wallpaper. His listeners were
entranced with the adventure of a group of martyrs who die
in defense of a lovely light-haired maiden. But when one
expelled member sought revenge by exposing the antics
of the secret society, young ringleader Grey was severely

punished by his stern father, and his manuscript was lost to posterity.

He gradually departed from his destructive mode and entered into acceptable social life. The family moved to Columbus, where his ability as a baseball pitcher won him a place in the University of Pennsylvania. Never a scholar, he nevertheless read widely—great authors as well as books on the technical aspects of writing. Expected to follow his father's profession, he worked toward a degree in dentistry while harboring a desire to be a writer. After graduation in 1896, he set up a dental practice in New York.

He disliked New York and he disliked dentistry. He longed for adventure, and a few articles on summer activities such as black bass fishing made their way into *Field and Stream*. But he wanted to write books.

The turning point came when his mother turned over to him an old notebook that had belonged to her grandfather; Ebenezer Zane had blazed a wilderness trail from West Virginia to Maysville, Kentucky—Zane's Trace—by which immigrant farmers made their way to the fertile Ohio Valley. A plaque in the Martins Ferry, Ohio, cemetery is inscribed to "the first permanent inhabitant of this part of the western world. . . ." It was Colonel Zane for whom Zanesville was named.

The heroic stories of his ancestors, who had played roles in the making of early American history, intrigued him. They were real people who had accomplished daring exploits—seen the Ohio River for the first time, lived in pioneer cabins, dined on wild turkey, dealt with Indians and hunters, built Fort Henry, known British traitors, and fought in the final victorious battle of the American Revolution.

He was particularly enthralled by the courage and heroism of Colonel Zane's sister Betty, who risked her life to

138

bring ammunition to Fort Henry when it was besieged by Indians and British in 1782. She ran through rifle fire, her apron filled with powder, to replenish ammunition supplies and save the fort.

He rewrote the diary account of her story in the form of a historical novel and was satisfied with the completed manuscript. But the publishers were not. Dozens refused *Betty Zane*. Grey persevered and convinced a wealthy patient to lend him money. Thus was his first novel published, at his own expense, by the Charles Francis Press in New York City.

The realization of the book, a symbol of promise, gave him the courage to relinquish both his profession and his name. He abandoned completely his career in dentistry, and he became Zane Grey. The book did not sell well in 1904 because the printer lacked the proper distribution channels, but Zane Gray left New York City and the distracting noise of elevated trains to live in the country and write. He had achieved a small success but was on the way.

An item in the local newspaper announcing his marriage in 1905 announced also that he was at work on another book. The newlyweds lived in Lackawaxen, Pennsylvania, and Dolly was a most encouraging partner. *The Spirit of the Border*, another historical novel based on his family's heroic deeds, appeared in 1906 on Dolly's insistence that he publish it despite their lack of funds. Indeed, money quickly ran out.

Just when fortune was at a low point, just when he might have returned to dental practice, Zane Grey met Buffalo Jones. Colonel C. J. Jones won his nickname by devoting himself to preservation of the American buffalo. He had come East to raise money for his conservation cause and captivated at least one member of the New York audience who heard him speak.

139

Grey, who had produced only two unimportant books and some articles in a five-year period, decided to go West and help in the fight against extinction of the buffalo. He would experience the adventurous life described by the plainsman—the riding and hunting, the storms and wild animals, the discoveries of Indian ruins and encounters with hostile Comanches—and write about it for eastern readers. The result was *The Last of the Plainsmen*.

With the manuscript complete, Buffalo Jones suggested that they present it personally to his friend Ripley Hitchcock of the editorial staff of Harper and Brothers. Although Mr. Hitchcock had previously rejected *Betty Zane, The Spirit of the Border*, and two other books, Zane's mentor knew that his friend would give this manuscript special treatment. He did. A few days afterwards he notified the writer to report to the editorial office in New York. The modicum of hope that Grey carried with him turned to utter devastation as he was told that Harper and Brothers had carefully considered the story and could not use it. Furthermore, added Hitchcock gratuitously, "I don't see anything in this to convince me you can write either narrative or fiction." Grey heard the cruel words and struggled out to the street in shock, under the burden of humiliation and total failure.

Somehow, inexplicably, despair turned to a deliberate determination to succeed. He met the crisis of failure by sending *The Last of the Plainsmen* from publisher to publisher, merely gathering a pile of rejection slips. And he wrote. He wrote and wrote, using as a backdrop for his tales of adventure the purple mountain majesty above the unfruited desert. Meanwhile, he lived with his family in utter poverty, sweeping away in winter the snow that came into the house through cracks in doors and windows. At last he completed *The Heritage of the Desert*.

Back he went to the office of Ripley Hitchcock. This time he placed the manuscript on the editor's desk and announced: "This is the kind of book I have been wanting to write for years, and I believe it is good. . . ." And home he went to wait. Again the notice came to see Mr. Hitchcock. But this time Hitchcock was sitting at his desk, smiling and holding out a piece of paper, a contract, the first of many he was to sign with Harper and Brothers, with whom he was to maintain a relationship for the rest of his life.

It would seem that he had arrived, but progress was not altogether smooth. Despite the success of his first romance, Harper refused the second. Grey carried the manuscript of *Riders of the Purple Sage* to the vice-president requesting that he read it himself. Both Mr. Duneka and his wife liked it, fortunately for the firm. It was published in 1912 and became a best seller—over 750,000 copies. From 1913 Grey was living comfortably on income from his books. His most popular novel sold over a million and a half copies by 1934.

He continued to seek adventure and went off on expeditions from which he sometimes derived material for his books. He hunted bear and elk, explored rivers and jungles, indulged in deep-sea fishing, and traveled to exotic far-off places around the world. Typically, he would produce two books and several articles a year. And Zane Grey remained on the list of America's most popular writers.

In the autumn of 1939, shortly after publication of his latest book, *Western Union*, Zane Grey died. Three more were published posthumously. What a legacy he left! His more than seventy books—nearly fifty novels as well as books for boys and non-fiction volumes—have sold over thirteen million copies.

His vast appeal to the masses underscores the distinct lack of sagacity and foresight of those early publishers who once again failed to recognize the potential success of a

141

would-be author. Zane Grey's continuing popularity, in both his books and films, testifies to the ongoing appeal of this enormously popular writer of Western novels.

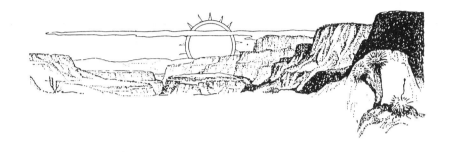